Pagan Portals
&
Shaman Pathways

...an ever-growing library of shared knowledge.

Moon Books has created two unique series where ~~~~ ~~ors
and practitioners come together to shar~ ~~~~
passion and expertise across the com~ ~~~~
would like to contribute to eithe~ ~~~~~ ~e
is simple and quick, just visit our ~~~~~ ~oks.net)
and click on Author Inquiry ~~~~~ ~ocess.

If you are a reader with a comment about a book or a suggestion
for a title we'd love to hear from you! You can find us at
facebook.com/MoonBooks or you can keep up to date with new
releases etc on our dedicated Portals page at facebook.com/
paganportalsandshamanpathways/

'Moon Books has achieved that rare feat of being synonymous
with top-quality authorship AND being endlessly innovative and
exciting.'
Kate Large, Pagan Dawn

Pagan Portals

Animal Magic, Rachel Patterson
An introduction to the world of animal magic and working with animal spirit guides

Australian Druidry, Julie Brett
Connect with the magic of the southern land, its seasons, animals, plants and spirits

Blacksmith Gods, Pete Jennings
Exploring dark folk tales and customs alongside the magic and myths of the blacksmith Gods through time and place

Brigid, Morgan Daimler
Meeting the Celtic Goddess of Poetry, Forge, and Healing Well

By Spellbook & Candle, Mélusine Draco
Why go to the bother of cursing, when a bottling or binding can be just as effective?

By Wolfsbane & Mandrake Root, Mélusine Draco
A study of poisonous plants, many of which have beneficial uses in both domestic medicine and magic

Candle Magic, Lucya Starza
Using candles in simple spells, seasonal rituals and essential craft techniques

Celtic Witchcraft, Mabh Savage
Wield winds of wyrd, dive into pools of wisdom; walk side by side with the Tuatha Dé Danann

Dancing with Nemetona, Joanna van der Hoeven
An in-depth look at a little-known Goddess who can help bring
peace and sanctuary into your life

Fairy Witchcraft, Morgan Daimler
A guidebook for those seeking a path that combines modern
Neopagan witchcraft with the older Celtic Fairy Faith

God-Speaking, Judith O'Grady
What can we do to save the planet? Three Rs are not enough.
Reduce, reuse, recycle...and religion

Gods and Goddesses of Ireland,
Meet the Gods and Goddesses of Pagan Ireland in myth and
modern practice

Grimalkyn: The Witch's Cat, Martha Gray
A mystical insight into the cat as a power animal

Hedge Riding, Harmonia Saille
The hedge is the symbolic boundary between the two worlds and
this book will teach you how to cross that hedge

Hedge Witchcraft, Harmonia Saille
Learning by experiencing is about trusting your instincts and
connecting with your inner spirit

Hekate, Vivienne Moss
The Goddess of Witches, Queen of Shades and Shadows, and
the ever-eternal Dark Muse haunts the pages of this poetic
devotional, enchanting those who love Her with the charm only
this Dark Goddess can bring

Herbs of the Sun, Moon and Planets, Steve Andrews
The planets that rule over herbs that grow on Earth

Hoodoo, Rachel Patterson
Learn about and experience the fascinating magical art of
Hoodoo

Irish Paganism, Morgan Daimler
Reconstructing the beliefs and practices of pre-Christian Irish
Paganism for the modern world

Kitchen Witchcraft, Rachel Patterson
Take a glimpse at the workings of a Kitchen Witch and share in
the crafts

Meditation, Rachel Patterson
An introduction to the beautiful world of meditation

Merlin: Once and Future Wizard, Elen Sentier
Merlin in history, Merlin in mythology, Merlin through the ages
and his continuing relevance

Moon Magic, Rachel Patterson
An introduction to working with the phases of the Moon

Nature Mystics, Rebecca Beattie
Tracing the literary origins of modern Paganism

Pan, Mélusine Draco
An historical, mythological and magical insight into the God Pan

Pathworking through Poetry, Fiona Tinker
Discover the esoteric knowledge in the works of Yeats, O'Sullivan
and other poets

Runes, Kylie Holmes
The Runes are a set of 24 symbols that are steeped in history, myths and legends. This book offers practical and accessible information for anyone to understand this ancient form of divination

Sacred Sex and Magick, Web PATH Center
Wrap up ecstasy in love to create powerful magick, spells and healing

Spirituality without Structure, Nimue Brown
The only meaningful spiritual journey is the one you consciously undertake

The Awen Alone, Joanna van der Hoeven
An introductory guide for the solitary Druid

The Cailleach, Rachel Patterson
Goddess of the ancestors, wisdom that comes with age, the weather, time, shape-shifting and winter

The Morrigan, Morgan Daimler
On shadowed wings and in raven's call, meet the ancient Irish Goddess of war, battle, prophecy, death, sovereignty, and magic

Urban Ovate, Brendan Howlin
Simple, accessible techniques to bring Druidry to the wider public

Your Faery Magic, Halo Quin
Tap into your Natural Magic and become the Fey you are

Zen Druidry, Joanna van der Hoeven
Zen teachings and Druidry combine to create a peaceful life path
that is completely dedicated to the here and now

Shaman Pathways

Aubry's Dog, Melusine Draco
A practical and essential guide to using canine magical energies

Black Horse White Horse, Mélusine Draco
Feel the power and freedom as Black Horse, White Horse guides
you down the magical path of this most noble animal

Celtic Chakras, Elen Sentier
Tread the British native shaman's path, explore the Goddess
hidden in the ancient stories; walk the Celtic chakra spiral
labyrinth

Druid Shaman, Danu Forest
A practical guide to Celtic shamanism with exercises and
techniques as well as traditional lore for exploring the Celtic
Otherworld

Elen of the Ways, Elen Sentier
British shamanism has largely been forgotten: the reindeer
Goddess of the ancient Boreal forest is shrouded in mystery...
follow her deer-trods to rediscover her old ways

Following the Deer Trods, Elen Sentier
A practical handbook for anyone wanting to begin the old British
paths. Follows on from Elen of the Ways

Trees of the Goddess, Elen Sentier
Work with the trees of the Goddess and the old ways of Britain

Way of the Faery Shaman, Flavia Kate Peters
Your practical insight into Faeries and the elements they engage
to unlock real magic that is waiting to help you

Web of Life, Yvonne Ryves
A new approach to using ancient ways in these contemporary
and often challenging times to weave your life path

Pagan Portals

Odin

Pagan Portals

Odin

Morgan Daimler

Winchester, UK
Washington, USA

First published by Moon Books, 2018
Moon Books is an imprint of John Hunt Publishing Ltd., Laurel House, Station Approach,
Alresford, Hants, SO24 9JH, UK
office1@jhpbooks.net
www.johnhuntpublishing.com
www.moon-books.net

For distributor details and how to order please visit the 'Ordering' section on our website.

ISBN: 978 1 78535 480 9
978 1 78535 481 6 (ebook)
Library of Congress Control Number: 2017940725

A CIP catalogue record for this book is available from the British Library.

Design: Stuart Davies

Printed and bound by CPI Group (UK) Ltd, Croydon, CR0 4YY, UK

We operate a distinctive and ethical publishing philosophy in
all areas of our business, from our global network of authors to
production and worldwide distribution.

Contents

Introduction   1

Chapter One: Who Is Odin?   7

Chapter Two: Odin in Mythology   27

Chapter Three: Odin Outside Norse Culture   35

Chapter Four: Symbols, Animals, and Items   41

Chapter Five: Odin in the Modern World   51

Chapter Six: Magic with Odin   67

Chapter Seven: Prayers and Poetry   77

Conclusion   84

Appendix A: Modern Media   85

Bibliography   86

This book is dedicated to Odin, inspirer of poets, gift-giver, gray-beard. God of wisdom accept this offering.
With thanks to all my friends in the northeast Heathen community, to my friends in the Troth, and to Stormlight Kindred.
Special thanks to Mayra who demonstrates so well what dedication looks like in action and always reminds me of what I need to hear when I need to hear it.

Special thanks as well to Ashley Bryner for the cover art

Author's Note

In writing this book I have tried to find a balance between academic sources and personal experiences. As someone who has been dedicated to Odin for almost a decade I want to share my own experience honoring him so that people can see at least one possible expression of Heathenry and Odin-worship in the modern world, but I also want to provide a strong academic resource for readers. I have tried to include an extensive bibliography and list a selection of other references that could potentially help readers connect to Odin in both intellectual and experiential ways. As with my previous books I am using American Psychological Association (APA) formatting for citations which means that after any quoted or paraphrased material you will see a set of parenthesis containing the author's last name and the date the book was published; this can be cross-referenced in the bibliography if you would like to know the source.

It would be impossible to include everything about Odin in a single book of this size; however, I have tried to include what I consider the most pertinent information. Ideally readers will be interested enough to continue researching and reading more, but if this is the only book on Odin that you read it should still give you a solid basic understanding of who Odin was and is. To accomplish this I am looking at sources spanning both Norse and German cultures, historic and modern, as well as books about Odin written by scholars as well as non-academics who feel a strong connection to him.

This book by nature will likely tend to focus on a more Heathen perspective, but it is written for anyone interested in Odin, regardless of religion or belief system. I don't think that a person's religion matters as much as the intent with which they approach the Gods and the effort they put into learning about them and connecting to them. So whether you are a Heathen, Asatruar, Reconstructionist, Neo-pagan, Wiccan, witch or any other variety of pagan or polytheist this book should still be useful to you. That said, however, my own personal experiences will tend to be framed within the context of my spirituality as an American Heathen.

Morgan Daimler, November 2016

Introduction

One of the most well-known and popular Norse Gods is without a doubt Odin. Honored by people across a wide array of different Pagan and Heathen traditions, called by many names, if you ask most people to think of a deity from the Norse pantheon Odin is the one they would likely mention (although Thor is probably a close second). A god who is well known yet still mysterious, who inspires both love and fear in those who acknowledge him, Odin's name still resonates with many people today.

Unlike some Germanic deities Odin is not an obscure God for whom we have only hints or a handful of references. In fact the opposite is true, Odin is found in so much material under so many different names that it can become difficult to keep it all straight and hard to ever feel as if you understand him, no matter how well studied you are. For people new to Heathenry, Asatru, or Norse paganism in general, getting to know Odin represents a real challenge and more so because not every source out there is trustworthy. This book then, as part of the Pagan Portals series, is meant to be a basic introductory text for those interested in Odin. This does not represent an end in anyone's journey to get to know this enigmatic deity, but rather a beginning and hopefully a useful reference.

Odin's name as we know it and as I am using it here is the Anglicized form of the Norse Oðinn which is ultimately derived from the proto-Germanic Woðanaz, itself from the proto-Indo-European root word wodeno meaning 'inspired, raging, or mad' (Harper, 2016). There are several related words in languages found in cultures who honored Odin, including the Norse óðr which means both 'voice' or 'poetry' and 'frenzy' and the Anglo-Saxon wod meaning 'fury' (Gundarsson, 2006). The root of wod has different connotations within the word we usually translate in English as fury, and these range from poetic inspiration to madness, however, even the concept of madness must be understood within context not as lunacy but as a king of divine ecstasy or possession (Kershaw, 2000). Looking at these root meanings for Odin's name can give us our first hints of his character, and indeed he is a God who inspires both creativity in poets and battle frenzy in warriors.

As with many things in paganism and academia there is an open-ended debate as to how closely connected some of the different cultural interpretations of Odin are. Is the Germanic Wodan the same being as the Icelandic Oðinn? Are they the same as the Anglo-Saxon Woden? Or are these similar names for deities who share a root in Indo-European culture but branched off into different beings? There is no definitive answer to these questions and the individual is left to decide for themselves how they will choose to understand Odin. For the purposes of this text the main focus will be on Odin as we understand him from the Icelandic material, but we look at Odin as he is understood in Germanic and Anglo-Saxon cultures as well.

In order to understand Odin, you need to have a basic understanding of Norse cosmology as well, because the two are strongly intertwined. It is difficult to discuss Odin without referencing things from the Norse worldview and belief system that honestly deserve a whole book of their own to explain, however, I am going to try to give something of a crash course here so that readers will have a basic idea of the concepts to move forward with. I highly recommend looking into the books in the bibliography at the end of this book for more information.

In the beginning we are told that there were two worlds: Niflheim which was a world of freezing ice and frigid rivers, and Muspelheim a world of primal fire. Between the two lay Ginungagap, a great expanse where the heat from the flames of Muspelheim met the ice of Niflheim and created a steaming fog. Over time this built up a coat of rime and out of this rime emerged two primordial beings: a giant named Ymir and a cow called Audumla. Ymir slept in Ginungigap and as he slept his body produced frost giants; meanwhile Audumla fed off the rime by licking at it, eventually licking free another being, Buri.

Buri's son and one of the giants, Bestla, produced three sons, including Odin. These three saw the frost giants proliferating from Ymir and decided to put an end to the primordial giant. From his body they fashioned our world called Midgard, and set everything in its place, from sky to sea, using his body to create everything. They created the dwarves [dvergr] and elves [alfar] as well as humans; there were still giants in the world, as some had survived Ymir's death and the resultant flood caused by his blood.

After this act of creation there were nine worlds according to Norse cosmology, although what exactly they were named varies slightly depending on source. I'll give them here as I know them. Our world is Midgard, or 'middle world' roughly. The Norse Gods, called Aesir, live in a world called Asgard which is joined to the other worlds by a rainbow bridge named Bifrost. There is another tribe of Gods called Vanir who live in a world called Vanaheim; three of these Vanic gods live among the Aesir as peace hostages after a war between the two groups and these are Njord and his children Freya and Freyr. The alfar live in Ljossalfheim, a world whose name means 'Light elf home' and the dwarves – or possibly the dark elves, depending on how you decide to interpret them[1] – live in Svartalfheim, or 'Black elf home'. The giants live in Jotunheim; a place that Thor and Loki sometimes travel to but otherwise is described as somewhat wild and dangerous. The dead live in Helheim[2], the land of the dead ruled by the Goddess Hella, one of Loki's children. And the two primal worlds of Niflheim and Muspelhiem still exist rounding out the eighth and ninth worlds. All of these worlds, according to lore, are arrayed on a world tree Yggdrasil which is itself complex.

The soul is seen as eternal in Heathenry and after death there are several options for where a soul can go. This is important to understand because much of Odin's prophecy related magic involved contacting the spirits of dead seeresses. Many people are also familiar with the idea of the battle dead going to Odin's hall, Valhalla (which we will discuss in more depth later), but there are a wide variety of options for a soul's destination. Some dead become mound dwellers; their souls going into the land. In *Eyrbyggja Saga* after Thorolfr's son drowns it is believed he goes into a hill on his father's land where he is welcomed with feasting (Eyrbyggja Saga, 1972). In *Gisla Saga* a man who is called a friend of Freyr dies and is buried in a mound and it is said that no frost will form on the hill because Freyr does not want frost to come between them (Gundarsson, 2006). In the *Voluspa* Odin goes to get an important prophecy from an ancient seer in a mound, something we also see Freya doing in another story. Additionally it has been suggested that some drokkalfar [mound elves] are the male dead of a family as the disir are the female dead (Gundarsson, 2006). Speaking of disir, it is entirely possible for a woman, after death, to become a disir, or idis, which is a specific type of spirit that watches over her family line (Gundarsson, 2006).

Reincarnation is also an old Heathen belief. A soul might be reborn within a family line and it's believed that naming a child after a deceased ancestor can mean the rebirth of that ancestor in the child (Ellis Davidson, 1968). In some cases a child might be born with similar marks or the appearance of a deceased family member which could indicate a soul relationship (Gundarsson, 2006). I have also heard it said, although I can't place the reference at the moment, that it was considered bad luck to name a child after a living relative for this reason.

It was prophesied that eventually a time would come called Ragnarok, or fate of the Gods, when the forces of entropy as embodied by the giants would overrun the world. This time would be foreshadowed by several events, beginning with three years of social chaos, with kinslaying and incest. Then there will fall a series of three harsh winters without summers in between; this time of endless cold would be called Fimbulvinter. After this set of six years the sun and moon will be swallowed by giants in the form of wolves, and the stars will disappear from the skies, then a great earthquake will shake Midgard. The Fenris wolf, who was bound because of his destructive potential, will break free, and his sibling the Midgard serpent will writhe in the sea causing a great tidal wave. The ship carrying the dead who will fight on the side of the giants will sail and the forces of Muspelheim, the giants of fire, will ride forth to fight against the Gods. The Aesir and Einherjar [heroic battle dead] will fight on one side and Loki and the Frost and Fire giants on the other. In the end all will be defeated and the world will be destroyed, but two humans will survive hidden in the World Tree and a handful of Gods – children of well-known Gods – will survive to begin anew.

Odin's story is interwoven in every aspect of this, from creation through to Ragnarok, and one of his main aims seems to be delaying the inevitability of the Gods' final fate as long as possible. Much of what he does is ultimately aimed at this goal, including his endless quest to gain more wisdom.

End Notes

1. There is some debate about whether the Svartalfar are properly elves or are another name for dwarves. Grimm suggests that the Svartalfar are a type of elf, however, Snorri seemed to see them as cognate with dwarves, and considered Svartalfheim home of the dwarves.

2. The Norse version of Hel, it should be noted, is vastly different from the Christian one. It is a place where most of the dead go, and so is home to most of the ancestors. The *Prose Edda* tells us that those who die of age or illness generally go to Hel's hall, while liars, murderers,

and oathbreakers go to Nastrond, both within Helheim (Young, 1964). Odin sent Loki's daughter Hel to Helheim to care for all the dead who came to her, and those who enter her realm belong to her. In the Edda, Helheim is described as gloomy and terrible, yet elsewhere in other stories, such as Baldr's Dream, it is described as a rich feasting hall, with ale ready to welcome guests (Bellows, 2007; Young, 1964).

Chapter One

Who Is Odin?

Odin I am called now, Yggr I was called before,
I was Thund before that,
Vak and Skilfing, Vafud and Hroptatyr,
Gaut and Jalk among the Gods,
Ofnir and Svafnir, all of which I think stem from me alone.
Grimnismal

Odin is a complex deity, one who we know from mythology and folklore, who appears across centuries and under many names. He appears prominently in Norse mythology taking on the role of leader of the Gods and as a figure who is instrumental in important situations. Odin created the worlds and humans with his two brothers, either named Vili and Ve or Heonur and Lodur depending on the version of the story. He works endlessly to gain wisdom to hold off the inevitable Ragnarok as long as possible and to prepare for it as best as possible. It was Odin who discovered the runes and gave them to the Gods, elves, dwarves, and humans; it was also Odin who tricked one of the giants (and the giant's daughter) to obtain Odroerir, the mead of poetry. Often his actions have widespread benefits for others but just as often his motives are obscure and difficult to fully understand.

Historically, Odin was a prominent and important God, with his statue being one of three main ones[1] at the temple in Uppsala, Sweden (Orchard, 1997). We see echoes of this importance even today in the name of one of our days of the week, Wednesday, or 'Woden's Day'. Many people are still drawn to Odin; among some pagans he is said to be quite active in the world, recruiting followers. Whether this is objectively true or not, he does seem to draw a strong following and to have gained a lot of popularity within Heathenry as well as, to some degree, within Paganism more generally. He is one of those deities that engenders strong feelings in people, for good or ill, and people do seem to find him fascinating.

In many ways he is a contradiction: a force of change that seeks to maintain the status quo, a God of wisdom that seeks to outwit others, a leader of the Gods who is known for wandering far from his home. The more you learn about Odin the more you will learn to accept the contradictions and to appreciate the layers to his myths.

Appearance

Odin is most often described as having only one eye, having sacrificed the other at Mimir's Well to gain more wisdom. Which eye is lost and which remains is unknown although many people have theories. Besides the missing eye, Odin is usually described as wearing blue or black, or a particular bluish-black called blár in Icelandic which was associated with mourning (Gundarsson, 2006).

In stories and art he often appears wearing a broad-rimmed hat or cloak with a hood, which may cover the side of his face with the missing eye. When he is not pictured with the hat, he may be shown with his hair covering that side of his face instead, although more modern depictions also favor an eye patch. He is also usually shown with a long beard; in recent artwork he may be either blond or gray haired. In mythology he may appear barefoot and in multicolored pants or in full armor, and when he bears a weapon it is a spear (Gundarsson, 2006). In the Gylfiganning he is described as riding out during Ragnarok dressed in *"a helmet of gold and a beautiful coat of mail and with his spear Gungnir"* (Young, 1964, p 87).

Powers and Associations

Odin, like any deity, can and will influence whatever he chooses to but there are particular areas that he is especially associated with. I might not go so far as to say that he is the god of these things in the traditional sense[2], but they are certainly things that he seems to have an especially keen interest in or knowledge of.

Poetry – Odin is known as the god of poets and poetry, although he is not the only one. It is Odin who possesses the mead of poetry, Odreorir, which gives inspiration, and Odin himself is known to inspire those who he chooses to. His direct inspiration is the sort that is rooted in the meaning of his name 'frenzy' and perhaps should best be understood in that context. He inspires through passion, both the obviously good sort that motivates the creation of epic writing and songs as well as the kind that drives warriors to rush headlong into battle.

Madness and Ecstasy – Odin is a God whose very name is rooted in the Old Norse word óðr 'furious' and Adam of Bremen said of him, "Woden id est furor" [Woden, that is madness] (Simek, 1993; translation Daimler, 2017). As with his aspect as a God of poets Odin's power as God of madness is rooted in his ability to inspire, in this case inspiring fury and frenzy. We see this in particular in the way he inspirers the Berserkers to battle-frenzy where they feel no pain and fight relentlessly. Simek suggest that ecstasy may have played a vital role in Odin's cults during the Heathen period (Simek, 1993). Kershaw posits that this madness was directly related to divine possession and ecstasy, and connects it to a type of inspiration (Kershaw, 2000).

Battle – Odin is a god of battle who can influence every aspect of battle from inspiring or stirring up wars, to encouraging warriors to fight to their utmost, to choosing who gains victory and who dies. Ynglinga Saga relates that Odin brought war to the world, and we are told that at the beginning of a fight a spear would be cast over the opposing army to dedicate it as a sacrifice to Odin (Simek, 1993). In a story in the Eddas where Freya obtains a magical necklace named Brisgingamen, Odin has Loki steal the necklace and will only return it if Freya causes two kings to go to war with each other (Crossley-Holland, 1981). Odin was also the one who could give or withhold victory depending on who he favored, and those who lost or were killed in battle were seen as having lost Odin's favor. In the Saga of King Hrolf Kraki, after King Hrolf and his men refuse a gift offered them by Odin in disguise and figure out it was in fact Odin offering it, one of the men comments, *"I suspect that we have not behaved very wisely in rejecting what we should have accepted. We may have denied ourselves victory."* (Byock, 1998, p. 69). During wars sacrifices were made to Odin for victory, both by pouring out drink and offering blood (Tourville-Petre, 1964).

The Dead – Odin's connection to the dead is a complex one. There is some suggestion that the main colors associated with him, particularly dark blue and blár, were colors of death that were symbolic of corpses (Gundarsson, 2006). His hall in Asgard was home to some of the dead, especially the heroic battle dead called Einherjar, and several of his by-names relate to the dead. Besides being associated with the battle dead he was also connected to those who died by hanging, and some of his other names refer to this, making him a god of the gallows. Additionally we see him seeking out the dead, as was mentioned above in the section on prophecy, in order to obtain information on future events, showing that he had the power and knowledge to call the dead forth from their burial mounds and communicate with them in Helhiem.

Magic – Odin is associated with several types of magic, most notably runic magic and seidhr, both of which will be discussed in greater depth in a later chapter. In the *Havamal* Odin discusses the various magical uses for runes that he knows and in *Baldrs Draumar* Odin is called the father of magic chants (Simek, 1993). We may also see an echo of his magical powers in his ability to shapeshift, as Odin is known to take multiple human disguises as well as the form of an eagle.

Wisdom – Odin as a God of wisdom could also be described as

a God of cunning, because he is associated with both knowledge for its own sake and with the clever use of it. It should be kept in mind that his pursuit of wisdom is ruthless, to the point that he hangs on the World Tree without sustenance for nine days to find the runes and gives an eye for a drink from Mimir's Well. Odin does not passively collect this knowledge either but rather uses what he gains, such as the knowledge of runes for magic, and the information in prophecies to affect the future. And no matter how much he knows he continues to seek more knowledge, trying to see whatever it might be in creation that he does not know (Bauschatz, 1982).

Prophecy – Odin has strong connections to prophecy, both as a deity who sees the future himself and as a God who is known in the stories to seek out those who can see the future to tell him what will come to pass. From his throne, Hlidskjalf, it is said that he can see all things, and we know that to obtain the prophecy about Ragnarok he traveled to the boundary of Helheim to speak to a dead Seeress. The practice of prophecy itself in a modern context is one that is strongly associated with him.

Odin by Any Other Name

Most Gods have a variety of different epithets attached to them and some have several different names which they are known by but none may have as many as Odin. If we look at all the different mythology and lore we find that Odin has more than 200 different names that he uses in different contexts or is known by in different places. Each of these names can be useful in helping us better understand who this enigmatic God is and I have also found it very useful to call on specific names of Odin when I need to honor or pray to different aspects of his energy. When we look at Odin by his different names, it is important to have at least a basic grasp of the meaning of each name; that meaning has tangible weight and value that affects the face of Odin which responds when we call. If you call on the Julfodr [Yule father] you will get a very different response than if you call on Ginnarr [Deceiver].

This is of course only a sample of his many names and should not be seen as an exhaustive list. Many of his names, like Bolverk (Evil Doer), relate to specific stories and it is a good idea to read those stories and understand the context of the story to understand the real meaning of the name. To this end each name I'm including is referenced so that a reader could find the original source to read it for themselves. If you are drawn to honor Odin I highly recommend learning something about a few of his many names in order to better understand him.

I will also add that I am no expert in Old Norse and all my suggestions for the meanings of these names should be checked against other sources. I suggest De Vries *Altnordisches Etymologisches Wörterbuch* and Egilsson's *Ordbog over det norsk-islandske Skjalde Sprog* as well as any good Icelandic or Old Norse dictionary, or book discussing Norse poetic kennings. Stephan Grundy's *Miscellaneous Studies Towards the Cult of Odinn* also offers some good discussions of many of Odin's names as does Kershaw's *The One-eyed God*.

Aldaföðr – *father of men* from Óðins nöfn, Vafþrúðnismál

Alföðr – *Allfather* from Óðins nöfn, Gylfaginning, Skáldskaparmál, Grímnismál

Algingautr – *aged God* from the Icelandic rune poem

Arnhöfði – *Eagle head* from Óðins nöfn

Atriðr – *attacking rider* from Óðins nöfn, Gylfaginning, Grímnismál

Auðun – *friend of wealth* from Óðins nöfn

Bági ulfs – *Enemy of the wolf* from Sonatorrek

Báleygr – *Fiery eyed* from Gylfaginning, Skáldskaparmál, Grímnismál

Biflindi – *Spear Shaker, Shield Shaker* from Óðins nöfn, Gylfaginning, Grímnismál

Bileygr – *Weak eye* from Óðins nöfn, Gylfaginning, Grímnismál

Blindr – *Blind* from Gylfaginning

Brúni, Brúnn – *Brown* from Óðins nöfn

Bölverkr – *Evil doer* from Óðins nöfn, Gylfaginning, Skáldskaparmál, Hávamál

Draugadróttinn – *Lord of the dead* from Ynglinga saga

Dresvarpr – *Spirit shedder* from Óðins nöfn

Ennibrattr – *Straight forehead* from Óðins nöfn

Eylúðr – *Always booming* from Óðins nöfn

Farmagnuðr, Farmögnuðr – *Trade empoweror* from Háleygjatal, Skáldskaparmál

Farmaguð, Farmatýr – *God of trade* from Gylfaginning, Skáldskaparmál, Grímnismál, Óðins nöfn

Fengr – *Fetcher or Catcher* from Óðins nöfn

Fimbultýr, Fimbultyr – *Mighty God* from Völuspá

Fimbulþulr, Fimbulthul – *Mighty Thuler* from Hávamál

Fjallgeiguðr – *Shape god* from Óðins nöfn

Fjölnir – *Many forms* from Grímnismál Gylfaginning, Óðins nöfn, Skíðaríma

Fjölsviðr – *Wide wisdom* from Gylfaginning, Grímnismál, Óðins nöfn

Fjörgynn – *Earth* from Lokasenna, Völuspá

Fornölvir – *Ancient Ölvir* from Óðins nöfn

Fráríðr, Fráríði – *One who rides forth* from Óðins nöfn

Friggjar angan – *Joy of Frigg* from Völuspá

Gagnráðr – *Victory counselor* from Vafþrúðnismál

Ganglari/Gangleri – *Wanderer or 'travel weary'* from Gylfaginning, Grímnismál, Óðins nöfn

Gangráðr – *Traveler* from Óðins nöfn

Gapþrosnir – *Gaping frenzy* from Óðins nöfn

Gautatýr, Gautatyr – *God of the Geats* from Skáldskaparmál, Eyvindr skáldaspillir's Hákonarmál

Gautr – *God* from Gylfaginning, Skáldskaparmál, Grímnismál, Óðins nöfn

Geiguðr – *Roamer* from Óðins nöfn

Geirlöðnir – *Spear inviter* from Óðins nöfn

Geirölnir – *Spear wielder* from Óðins nöfn

Geirs Drotinn – *Spear Shaker* from Egil's Saga

Ginnarr – *Deceiver* from Óðins nöfn

Gizurr – *Riddler* from Óðins nöfn

Gestumblindi – *Blind* Guest from Hervarar saga, þulur, Óðins nöfn

Glapsviðr – *Skilled in beguiling* from Gylfaginning, Grímnismál, Óðins nöfn

Göllnir – *Yeller* from Óðins nöfn

Göndlir/Gondlir – *Wand bearer* from Gylfaginning, Grímnismál, Óðins nöfn

Grímnir – *Masked One* Gylfaginning, Grímnismál, Óðins nöfn

Grímr – *Grim* from Gylfaginning, Grímnismál, Óðins nöfn

Gungnis Vafadr – *Gungnir's Shaker* from a 9th-century poetic reference (Simek, 1993).

Gunnblindi – *War blinder* Óðins nöfn

Hagvirkr – *Skillful worker* from Óðins nöfn

Hangadróttinn – *Lord of the hanged* from Ynglinga saga

Hangaguð/Hangatýr – *God of the Hanged* from Gylfaginning, Skáldskaparmál

Haptaguð/Haptagud – *God of Prisoners* from Gylfaginning

Hárbarðr/Harbard – *Gray Beard* from Gylfaginning, Grímnismál, Hárbardsljód, Óðins nöfn

Hárr – *High* from Gylfaginning, Grímnismál, Óðins nöfn

Hávi/Hovi – *High One* from Hávamál, Óðins nöfn

Helblindi – *Death blinder/Hel blinder* from Gylfaginning, Grímnismál

Hengikeptr, Hengikjopt – *Hang jaw* from Óðins nöfn

Herblindi – *Host blinder* from Óðins nöfn

Herföðr/Herjaföðr – *Father of warriors* from Gylfaginning, Völuspá Grímnismál, Óðins nöfn

Herjan – *Battle lord* from Gylfaginning, Grímnismál, Óðins nöfn, Völuspá

Herteitr – *Battle glad* from Gylfaginning, Grímnismál, Óðins nöfn

Hertýr – *God of warriors* from Skáldskaparmál

Hjálmberi – *Helmet bearer* from Gylfaginning, Grímnismál, þulur, Óðins nöfn

Hjarrandi – *Screamer* from Óðins nöfn

Hléfreyr – *Lord of rest* from Óðins nöfn

Hleifruðr – *Peace breaker* from Óðins nöfn

Hnikarr/Hnikar – *Inciter* from Gylfaginning, Grímnismál, Reginsmál, Óðins nöfn

Hnikuðr – *Inciter* from Gylfaginning, Grímnismál, Óðins nöfn

Hrafnaguð – *Raven God* from Gylfaginning

Hrami – *Ripper* from Óðins nöfn

Hrjóðr – *Roarer* from Óðins nöfn

Hropt – *Shouter* from Gylfaginning, Hávamál, Grímnismál, Sigrdrífumál, Óðins nöfn, Völuspá

Hrosshársgrani – *Horse hair beard* Óðins nöfn

Hvatmóðr – *Brisk Courage or Active Mind* from Óðins nöfn

Hveðrungr – *Stormer* from Óðins nöfn

Jafnhárr – *Equally high* from Gylfaginning, Grímnismál, Óðins nöfn

Jálkr – *Gelding* from Gylfaginning, Grímnismál, Óðins nöfn

Jólnir/Jölnir – *Yule God* from Óðins nöfn

Jölföðr – *Yule father* from Óðins nöfn

Jörmunr – *The mighty one* from Óðins nöfn,

Kjalarr/Kjalar – literally *'Keel'* from Gylfaginning, Skáldskaparmál, Grímnismál, Óðins nöfn

Langbarðr – *Long Beard* from Óðins nöfn

Löndungr/Loðungr – *Shaggy Cloak* from Óðins nöfn

Njótr – *Enjoyer* from Óðins nöfn

Ófnir – *Inciter* from Óðins nöfn

Olgr – *Hawk* from Óðins nöfn

Ómi/Omi – *Resonant voice* from Gylfaginning, Grímnismál, Óðins nöfn

15

Óski – *Wish-giver* from Gylfaginning, Grímnismál, Óðins nöfn

Rögnir – *Ruler of the Gods/warriors* from Óðins nöfn

Saðr/Sadr, Sannr – *Truthful, True* from Gylfaginning, Grímnismál, Óðins nöfn

Sanngetall – *Truth seeker* from Gylfaginning, Grímnismál, Óðins nöfn

Síðhöttr – *Low hat* from Gylfaginning, Grímnismál, Óðins nöfn

· Síðskeggr – *Low beard* from Gylfaginning, Grímnismál, þulur, Óðins nöfn

Sigðir – *Victory giver* from Óðins nöfn

Sigföðr – *Father of victory* from Gylfaginning, Völuspá, Grímnismál, Óðins nöfn

Siggautr – *Victory God* from Óðins nöfn

Sigmundr – *Victory protection* from Óðins nöfn

Sigtryggr – *Victory-sure* from Óðins nöfn

Sigtýr – *God of Victory* from Skáldskaparmál,

Sigþrór – *Strong in victory* from Óðins nöfn

Skilfingr – *Chief* from Gylfaginning, Grímnismál, Óðins nöfn

Skollvaldr – *Ruler of treachery* from Óðins nöfn

Sváfnir – *Sleep giver* from Gylfaginning, Grímnismál, Óðins nöfn

Sviðrir/Svidrir – *Wise one* from Gylfaginning, Grímnismál, Óðins nöfn

Sviðuðr – *One who brings rest* from Óðins nöfn

Sviðurr/Svidur – *Spear God* from Gylfaginning, Skáldskaparmál, Grímnismál, Óðins nöfn

Svipall – *Shape-shifter* Gylfaginning, Grímnismál, Óðins nöfn

Svölnir /Svolnir – *Cooler* from Skáldskaparmál, Óðins nöfn

Tveggi – *Double* from Óðins nöfn, Völuspá

Tvíblindi – *Twice blind* from Óðins nöfn

Þekkr/Thekk – *Enduring One or Beloved* from Gylfaginning, Grímnismál, Óðins nöfn

Þrasarr – *Quarreler* from Óðins nöfn

Þriði/Thriggi – *Third* from Gylfaginning, Skáldskaparmál, Grímnismál, Óðins nöfn

Þrór/Thror – *Successful* from Gylfaginning, Grímnismál, Óðins nöfn

Þróttr/Thrott – *Strength* from Glymdrápa

Þuðr, Thud, Thunn – *Thin* from Gylfaginning, Óðins nöfn

Þundr/Thundr – *Rumbler* from Gylfaginning, Hávamál, Grímnismál, Óðins nöfn

Uðr/Unn – *Beloved* from Gylfaginning, Grímnismál, Óðins nöfn

Váfuðr – *Wind One* from Gylfaginning, Skáldskaparmál, Grímnismál

Vakr – *Wakeful from* Gylfaginning, Grímnismál, Óðins nöfn

Valföðr – *Father of the slain* from Gylfaginning, Völuspá Grímnismál Óðins nöfn

Valgautr – *God of the slain* from Óðins nöfn

Vegtam – *Wanderer or Road Traveler* from Baldrs draumar

Veratýr – *God of men* from Gylfaginning, Óðins nöfn

Viðrir/Vidrir – *Weather-controller* from Gylfaginning, Skáldskaparmál, Lokasenna

Viðrímnir – *Screamer* from Óðins nöfn

Viðurr Vidur – *Slayer* from Gylfaginning, Grímnismál, Óðins nöfn, Karlevi Runestone

Vingnir – *Swinger or Turner* from Óðins nöfn

Vófuðr – *Dangler* from Óðins nöfn

Yggr – *Terrifying One* Gylfaginning, Völuspá, Grímnismál, Óðins nöfn

Ýjungr/Ýrungr – *Stormer* Óðins nöfn

Family, Lovers, and Others

Odin has a large and complex family as well as several important associates not directly related by blood, and each of the deities associated closely with him is usually significant in the mythology.

The *Prose Edda* explains his by-name of 'All Father' by saying that he was *"the father of all the gods and men and of everything that he and his power created"* (Young, 1964, p. 37). This reinforces both his centrality in mythology and his strong connections to many of the Gods and to humanity at large.

His mother is the giantess Bestla and his father is Bur, the son of the primordial being Buri who was licked from the ice of the great frozen waste by the cow Audumla. His maternal uncle is the giant Mimir, who possesses one of three wells at the roots of the world tree, and who was sent to the Vanir as a peace hostage along with one of Odin's brothers. Unfortunately that ended badly and Mimir was beheaded after the Vanic gods felt he was tricking them by making them believe Odin's brother was wise when he was not. Odin preserved Mimir's head with magic and herbs and it still speaks its wisdom. His has two brothers, named alternately Vili and Ve or Heonir and Lodur.

Frigga – Odin's wife and the mother of his son Baldur. Frigga was a major Goddess in the Norse pantheon, able to see the future as Odin could though lore says she didn't speak of what she saw. There are some strong hints in related material that she was a sovereignty goddess, and in one story when Odin goes off wandering and is gone for too long his brothers assume rulership and marry Frigga in his place. When he returns he reclaims both his throne and his wife, hinting at her role in granting authority to rule.

The goddess Frigga is Odin's wife, but he is also known to have dalliances with many others in the mythology. These include an array of different giantesses, many of whom gave him children.

Jord – also called Fjorgyn, her name means 'earth' and she is considered to be a primordial earth Goddess. Her parents are Nott [night] and Anarr, and she is most well known in myth as Thor's mother, although she may have held an earlier significance on her own as a primordial earth deity (Simek, 1993).

Gunnlod – the daughter of the giant Suttungr, Gunnlod was the guardian of the mead of poetry. Odin was denied the mead by her father so he snuck into the cave where Gunnlod was and stayed with her for three nights to earn three sips of the mead. When given access to the mead, he drained the three containers the mead was in with three draughts and fled in the form of an eagle. Gunnlod's name means 'invitation to battle' and Simek conjectures that she is reminiscent of a Valkyrie who gives out mead (Simek, 1993).

Rind – Rind is described as both one of the Goddesses of the Aesir and also a mortal king's daughter in different sources where she is named either Rindr or Rinda respectively. After Baldur's death Odin hears a prophecy that only his son by Rind can avenge Baldur, so he sets out to find and woo her, however, Rind has no interest in his attention (Simek, 1993). He approaches her in four different disguises, the first three attempting to court her and the fourth as a healing woman who promises to cure the madness brought her by Odin (Simek, 1993). In this final disguise he is able to force himself on the unwilling woman and his son Vali is conceived.

Skadhi – daughter of the giant Thjazi and at one point wife of the Vanic God Njord; her father chased Loki into Asgard and was killed by the Gods, so she went there herself in order to claim weregild for his death. As a result of this she was married to Njord, but the two could not reconcile their different natures, with Skadhi preferring to live in the wintery mountains and Njord preferring the seashore. Skadhi was a giantess later accepted among the Aesir. She is often viewed as a Goddess of the winter and skills associated with it, such as skiing. After leaving Njord the *Ynglinga Saga* tells us that she and Odin became lovers and she had several children by him, at least one of whom, Earl Hakon, founded a line of human nobles (Simek, 1993).

One of Odin's many heiti, or by-names, is 'All Father' and while it may have different contexts it can certainly be taken rather literally as he is a very prolific deity. In the mythology he is said to not only have fathered a variety of Gods but also different human kings. Not all of his divine children are with his wife Frigga, contributing to Odin's reputation as a deity who was fond of female companionship. As with most things in mythology there can be variances between sources as to who parented whom, so we sometimes see one source claiming Odin was a particular being's father while another myth claims a different father for that same deity. For our purposes here I'm just going to list anyone who is said to be his child in a source, but if you are interested I do suggest further research on each of them. Many of his children are significant deities in their own right and worth exploring in more depth.

Thor

Odin's son with the Goddess Jord [literally earth]; Thor was one of the most popular Gods in Norse culture. He was also said to be Odin's first son (Young, 1964). He is featured often in many myths, which describe his adventures protecting the world by fighting against the forces of entropy as embodied by the more dangerous Giants. His wife is the Goddess Sif and he has three children, two sons Magni and Modi, and a daughter Thrudr, and his step son is the God Ullr.

Thor often travels to Midgard in a chariot pulled by two goats and his most common companion on his travels is Loki. Although Thor is sometimes viewed as oafish he is just as clever as his father and in one story he saves his daughter from having to marry a dwarf by challenging him to a game of wits and keeping him engaged until the sun rises and the dwarf is turned to stone.

Thor's greatest weapon was his hammer Mjolnir, a treasure obtained from the dwarves by Loki. Thor was an immensely popular God during the pre-Christian period and he was often viewed as the God of the common man, in contrast to Odin who was the God of the nobility and poets.

Baldur

According to the *Gylfaginning*, Baldr is Odin's second son; he is a very important deity in one of the most well-known stories from the Eddas, *Bauldrs Draumr*, and is often described as very beautiful and much loved. His mother is Odin's wife Frigga, his wife is the Goddess Nanna and his son is the justice deity Forseti (Simek, 1993).

In mythology, Baldur has a troubling dream of his own death. His mother then secures promises from everything, living and inanimate, not to bring any harm to him but she forgets to ask the mistletoe. Loki learns about this oversight and when he sees the Gods entertaining themselves by throwing things at Baldur, who cannot be hurt, he presses a mistletoe dart into the hands of Hodur, who is blind. The blind God throws the dart and fatally wounds Baldur. Despite efforts by Frigga and Odin to secure his release from Helheim, Baldur remains there waiting Ragnarok and the re-birth of the world.

At his funeral his wife Nanna died of grief and was cremated with him on his pyre; Odin gave his arm ring Draupnir to Baldur at his funeral (Simek, 1993). He also whispered something into his son's ear, although what is unknown.

Hodur

By some accounts also a son of Odin, although this is disputed in different versions of the mythology (Simek, 1993). He is described in the *Prose Edda* as being immensely strong (Young, 1964). He is a blind deity often associated with winter, and it is his hand that casts the ill-fated mistletoe that kills Baldur.

Hermod

Odin's son, an obscure deity. It is Hermod who rides to Helhiem to try to convince Hella on Odin and Frigga's behalf to free Baldur after he is killed. Hella agrees on the single condition that every living thing cry for Baldur's death, but one giantess named Thokk refuses. Because Thokk would not cry for him, Baldur remains in Helhiem with the dead and Hermod's mission fails.

Vidur

Said in some sources to be Odin's son and in others to be the son of a giant, Vidur will avenge Odin's death by killing the Fenris wolf. Vidur, along with his half-brother Vali and Thor's two sons Magni and Modi, will survive Ragnarok and help rebuild the world (Simek, 1993). Snorri calls him a silent God and says that he is nearly as strong as Thor (Young, 1964).

Bragi

Odin's son by an unnamed mother; I have seen it suggested in conversation that his mother was the giantess Gunnlod. His name is related to the Norse word for poetry, bragr, and he is unsurprisingly a God of poetry and eloquence (Simek, 1993). His wife is the Goddess Idunna.

Vali

Odin's son with the giantess Rind; Vali's birth was prophesied and intentionally brought about by Odin in order to avenge the death of his son Baldur. According to myth Vali avenged his half-brother's death when he himself was only one day old (Simek, 1993). Other than the story of his conception and accomplishing this single feat we have no other stories relating to him, although in the *Vafthrudnismal* it is said that he is one of the Gods who will survive Ragnarok and help build the new world after the old is destroyed (Simek, 1993). Snorri says of him that he is "bold in battle and a very good shot" (Young, 1964, p55).

Loki

Loki is one of, possibly the, most controversial figures in modern Heathenry. There are people who will not participate in rituals where Loki is being invoked, and there are others who will always offer something to him if Odin is being offered to. Loki is a complex and complicated figure in mythology, a trickster who often causes the Aesir significant problems but also brings them great gifts and advantages when he gets them out of those same problems.

Loki is the son of two giants, Laufey and Farbauti, but is also numbered among the Aesir in the Eddas. He is the father of three very significant beings: the world serpent Jormungandr, the wolf Fenris who will kill Odin at Ragnarok, and Hella, the goddess who rules Hellheim where the dead go. We learn in the Lokasenna, he is Odin's blood brother, and in that story we are told that Odin had taken an oath never to drink unless Loki was given a drink as well.

Valkyries

Not related to Odin by blood but strongly associated with him are the Valkyries, mythic warrior women who occupied a liminal place between the dead and the Gods. Their name is from the Old Norse word 'Valkyrjar' which is made up of the words 'valr' – the battlefield dead – and 'kjósa', to choose, giving us the meaning 'choosers of the battle slain' (Simek, 1993). In the *Prose Edda* it says of the Valkyries, "Odin sends them to every battle, and they choose death for the men destined to die, and award victory." (Young, 1964, p61). The Valkyries were said to control both who died in battle and where they went after death, with half going to Freya's hall Sessrumnir and the other half to Odin's hall. They were also said to choose who would gain victory or who would lose in a battle and who would be killed at Odin's command. They have long been closely associated with Odin, even being called *'Odins meyar'* [Odin's girls], and were understood as beings who did his will (Simek, 1993). The overall understanding of who and what the Valkyries were did change over time, however, with the oldest understanding of them reflecting a fiercer nature more strongly connected to the dead which later seemed to soften and become more human, even allowing for romance with epic heroes (Simek, 1993).

Einherjar

The Einherjar are great warriors, the souls of the battle dead collected by the Valkyries and brought to Odin's hall. It is said in the *Prose Edda* that Odin is called Valfather [father of the slain] because all who die in battle are his adopted sons (Young, 1964). These warriors are brought to Valhalla where they spend the day fighting and the night feasting, with each day repeating as the one before. The word 'einherjar' means "those who fight alone" (Simek, 1993). The Einherjar are essential to both Odin and to humanity at large as they will fight for the gods (and us) at Ragnarok against the forces of entropy.

Odin in My Life – A God of Many Names

I have several specific by-names of Odin that I call on regularly but I want to be very clear that these are all names for a single god – Odin – not different Gods. The best analogy for this might be to compare it to the use of nicknames. I honor Odin as one being but I choose different heiti (by-names or nicknames) for him in different contexts. I have found that this is a good way to connect to more specific aspects or energies associated with Odin.

In stories in the *Gylfaginning* and *Grímnismál* Odin appears as Harbard, meaning Gray Beard. In this guise he is a ferryman who challenges Thor by refusing to ferry him across a river and insulting him. When I am feeling challenged by Odin this is the name I use for him. This is also the name I call on and pray to in challenging times or when I am trying to maintain my self-control when being confronted by difficult people.

In Óðins nöfn we are told that Odin is also known as Jölföðr, meaning Yule father. My family honors Odin by this name every Yule and we see him as the one who brings gifts to the children. I'm not saying Odin is Santa Claus but I will say that I see the Yule Father as one of Odin's most benevolent and kind forms, where he reinforces reciprocity by encouraging the giving of gifts and the celebration of joy and fellowship in the darkest time of the year.

Oski, God of Wishes and things wished, is a name for Odin in the *Gylfaginning* and *Grímnismál*. I pray to him sometimes for inspiration and often for luck. He always expects a gift for a gift, in my experience, but he is generous with his giving. I have prayed and offered to Oski several times in dire financial circumstances and always had a positive outcome, although never quite in an expected form.

In *Baldr's Draumar* Odin goes by the name Vegtam meaning Wanderer or Way-tamer. I call on him by this name especially for seidhr work because I see him as Odin who travels the nine worlds and journeys to the realm of the dead. As a seidhkona this resonates with me and I find this name for Odin works really well for me when I am doing those same things myself.

There are a few other names I also use regularly for Odin. One from the *Gylfaginning* is Hrafnagud, meaning Raven God. I tend to use this one when doing divination or receiving omens more generally and almost always when I see ravens or crows I feel are associated with Odin. Another which is found in both the *Gylfaginning* and the *Skaldaparmal* is Vidrir, meaning Stormer; I tend to associate this one with Odin of the Wild Hunt. I use this name when storms pass by, when I feel the Wild Hunt near, or when I am calling on Odin in the context of the Leader of the Hunt. I use the name Hroptatyr, or Sage, from the *Gylfaginning* when I am honoring Odin as a wise teacher or offering to him in the context of learning. I use this one often in relation to the runes. Finally for healing work I pray to him as Veratyr, God of Men, a name from both the *Gylfaginning* and Óðins nöfn.

End Notes

1. The other two statues were Thor and Freyr, who we know were also very popular in pre-Christian Norse religion.

2. By this I mean that people tend to understand Gods as 'the God of X' and then pigeonhole the deity into that role. However, that approach doesn't work especially well with the Norse pantheon (or several other pantheons for that matter) because they have a flexibility to them in what they can and will do. There is a great deal of cross-over between the different Gods, and overlap, in who is the God of what, so that we see Odin as a God who foresees the future but we see Frigga doing this as well. Odin is a God of warriors, especially berserkers, but Thor is also a God of warriors, although perhaps of a different sort. In this way there is no true specialization in the Norse pantheon, only those who favor certain purviews over others.

Chapter Two

Odin in Mythology

He lives forever and ever, and rules over the whole kingdom and governs all things great and small.
Gylfiganning

Odin is often called the God of poets so it shouldn't be surprising that he appears often in the myths and tales we have in writing, which were mostly composed or written by the poets. Reading the mythology gives us the impression that Odin was the primary deity of the Norse, and he may have been, but we should also keep in mind that this impression may be skewed by the writers. We know that Thor and Freyr were also much loved and often worshipped, for example, and that should be kept in mind when looking at Odin's place in the myths.

In the *Prose Edda*

The *Prose Edda* was written by Snorri Sturluson in the early 13th century and provides us with a great deal of what we know about Icelandic and Norse mythology. It begins by trying to place the Norse Gods in a historic context as well as relating them to Classical mythology. In this guise the introduction of the text describes the Aesir as humans living in Troy, and claims that Odin and his wife were skilled in prophecy and learned by this means that if they traveled to the north they would be greatly revered and gain fame. In this way the Gods are euhemerized at the start of the tale into mere humans, although the work then goes on to relate what are clearly mythic tales.

The first story in the *Prose Edda* is the *Gylfiganning* or Deluding of Gylfi. It tells the story of a Swedish king who travels to Asgard after encountering the Goddess Gefjon. There he engages in a long discourse with Odin, in the form of a question-and-answer conversation, with Gylfi asking about how the world was created and who the Gods are.

First Odin relates that he is the most powerful of all the Gods and gives a list of a dozen names that he is called. Then at Gylfi's prompting he explains that during the creation of the world Odin and his two brothers kill the primordial giant Ymir, whose body was producing frost giants, and dismember him to create the world and beings within it. Afterwards they come across two pieces of wood, an ash and elm, and from these they make the first two humans. Odin's brothers give the wood form and flesh, but he is the one who breathes life and soul into them. He then tells Gylfi how he arranged all things in the world, including setting the giantess Night and her half-Aesir son Day into the sky, as well as placing the brother and sister Moon and Sun into the sky to travel the heavens with Night and Day (Young, 1964). With further questioning Odin relates how he structured things in Asgard and how he gave an eye at Mimir's well to drink from its waters, which give wisdom and knowledge.

Odin goes on to tell Gylfi that there are 12 main Gods in Asgard and 12 Goddesses, listing them and describing something about each one, beginning with himself. He then describes the details about the Valkyries and Einherjar, what the halls of the Gods are like in Asgard, and different stories about the Gods and how they acquired their most well-known treasures.

Then Odin relates Baldur's dream of his death and the attempts made by Odin to find out if there was any truth to the dreams and Frigga's attempts to prevent it coming to pass. When this resulted in the death occurring, Frigga tried to have him returned from Helheim, but without success. This led to Loki being hunted down and punished, as he was ultimately blamed for Baldur's death and Frigga's failure to bring him back.

Finally Odin tells Gylfi about Ragnarok, or the prophecy of the fate of the Gods. According to this prophecy Odin will eventually face one of Loki's children, Fenris, an enormous wolf who was bound by the Gods, and the wolf will kill him. After the world has been destroyed, it will be remade by the few Gods who survive and things will begin anew. In this way the *Gylfiganning* relates everything about the Gods from creation to destruction, narrated by Odin.

In the *Poetic Edda*

Odin has a significant role in many of the poems in the *Poetic Edda*, a collection which was written in the 13th century by Snorri Sturluson and that can be found in multiple English translations. The *Poetic Edda* contains a series of poems which relate important stories from Norse mythology, including how the worlds were created, an explanation of who the different Gods are, some of their adventures, and a prophecy of how the world will end. In many of these poems Odin acts as the instigator or a main character, and he is often the one who is pivotal in creating something or obtaining a necessary item or piece of information.

The first story in the *Poetic Edda* is the *Voluspa*, or Seeress's Prophecy. In this we see Odin questioning an ancient seeress, who relates to him the creation and history of the Gods and all the worlds and follows through to predicting Ragnarok. It includes a refrain that is still sometimes used by modern Heathens who practice prophecy, 'would you know more, or what?'.

One of the most well-known, if not the most well-known, pieces in the *Poetic Edda* is the *Havamal*, or the Saying of the High One. This is a recitation of wisdom sayings given by Odin and includes an array of things from the prosaic to the esoteric. We hear about Odin's infiltration of Suttung's hall and wooing of Gunnlod to gain the mead of poetry. It is in the *Havamal* that we learn of Odin's finding the runes and he also mentions 18, although not by name, and their magical uses.

In the *Vafthrudnismal*, or Vafthrudnir's Sayings, we find Odin traveling disguised as a poor wanderer to test his knowledge against the giant Vafthrudnir. The two engage in a game of riddles, each asking the other questions to test their knowledge. Finally the wanderer asks the giant what it was that Odin whispered in Baldur's ear on his funeral pyre, and the giant realizes who it really is that he has been talking with and admits defeat, saying, "*I've been contending with Odin in wisdom; you'll always be the wisest of beings.*" (Larrington, 1996, p49).

In the *Griminsmal*, the Sayings of Grimnir, we see Odin and Frigga contesting over two humans that they had fostered; the two boys had been shipwrecked one fall and Odin and Frigga disguised as an elderly couple had raised them. Odin favored the younger while Frigga favored the older, but when they sent the boys back to their home in the spring Odin told his foster son how to trick his brother to send him back out to sea, thus ensuring the younger became king. When he gloated about his foster son's success to Frigga she accused the man of stinginess, and Odin traveled disguised as a traveler named Grimnir to prove her wrong. Instead he was taken by the king and bound between two pillars, near bright fires, until after nine nights he revealed his identity and announced that only the king's son Agnar, who had given him a drink, would have Odin's favor.

In the *Hardbardsljod*, or Song of Harbard, we see Odin disguised as a ferryman named Harbard refusing to ferry Thor across a river. The two stand on opposite sides of the water trading insults until Thor finally gives up and asks for directions on where to travel if the ferryman won't bring him over.

In the *Lokasenna*, or Loki's Quarrel, we see Loki forcing his way into a party the Gods are holding in Aegir's hall. They are going to refuse him, Bragi saying he will never have a seat in Aegir's hall, but Loki is quick to remind Odin that they are blood-brothers and the Odin had said he "*would never drink ale unless it was brought to both of us*" (Larrington, 1996, p87). Loki is allowed in and proceeds to insult each God and Goddess in turn, including Odin who he accuses of giving victory to the undeserving and of practicing womanly forms of magic[1]. The story ends when Thor arrives and threatens Loki who responds by setting fire to the hall.

In the *Reginsmal*, or Lay of Regin, we learn of Odin's connection to the Volsungs, and how the actions of Odin and Loki caused the curse of Andvari's ring which would be pivotal in the saga of the Volsungs. The hero Sigurd later meets Odin disguised as an old man named Hnikar, and asks the disguised God about battle omens; Odin gives him a series of omens and their interpretations.

The final text in the *Poetic Edda* that mentions Odin is a version of *Baldurs Draumar*, Baldur's Dream, which was also written about in the *Prose Edda*.

In the Sagas

Odin appears in several places in the various Sagas, sometimes as a God and sometimes as a euhemerized human but still with clear echoes of the deity. He may show up in disguise, only later to be revealed as Odin, or he may appear as a figure being prayed to by characters within the story.

In the *Ynglinga Saga* Odin is re-cast as a mortal warrior, but the story that is told is similar to that of the Eddas, with the Gods being called the tribe of the Aesir who are said to live in Asgard. The story tells of 12 main 'priests' who seem to be cognate to the 12 main Gods of the Aesir, and Odin is described as so successful a warrior in battle that other warriors prayed to him. He is also said to have left his kingdom to wander the world during which time his wife Frigga took both his brothers to her bed, and they ruled in Odin's stead until he returned.

In the *Volsunga Saga* Odin appears to answer the prayer of King Rerir and his wife who are childless. Through both Frigga and Odin's intervention, a Valkyrie is sent to give the king an apple which causes the conception of his son. He continues to appear throughout the tale at key points to guide the fate of this family, sometimes in very direct ways.

The cursed ring that causes much of the plot is brought about by the actions of Odin, Loki, and Hoenir. These gods kill an otter while fishing which is actually a man named Otr shape-changed; to pay the weregild for this act they must cover his otter pelt inside and out with gold. Odin and Hoenir are held hostage and Loki is sent out to find the gold, and in so doing he extorts it from a dwarf named Andvari, who subsequently curses a ring among the horde.

In the *Saga of King Hrolf Kraki* Odin appears and aids the king disguised as a one-eyed farmer named Hrani, welcoming the King and his men as guests at his farm and giving them good advice which the king accepts. On their second meeting, however, when Odin offers the king armor the king disparages it and refuses; Odin is greatly offended. Only after riding away do King Hrolf and his men realize that the farmer was Odin and turn around to apologize, fearing they have cost themselves victory, but they find that the farmer and his farm have disappeared (Byock, 1998).

In the *Hakonarmal*, Lay of Hakon, we see Odin sending his Valkyries out to bring King Hakon to Vahalla from the battlefield. Hakon travels with the Valkyries and is met by Bragi and Hermod, who reassure him when he uneasy about entering Odin's hall. Hakon had died a Christian, but had not defiled any Heathen sites and had died believing in the old gods, so he is welcomed into Valhalla with his family and the Einherjar (Adalsteinsson, 1998).

Miscellaneous

In the *Historia Longobardorum* there is a story of Odin and Frigga, by the names of Wodan and Frea, which says that Odin favored one side and Frigga the other; eventually the side Frigga favored won after she tricked Odin into giving them victory (Simek, 1993).

Odin in My life

I started looking into Heathenry in late 2005 and by early 2006 I felt a strong sense of presence around myself. Having been a polytheist at that point for over a decade I was more curious than alarmed and assumed it was probably a deity from the new pantheon I was studying, but I had no idea which one.

The feeling is hard to describe but generally was a sense of interest and fondness. Not knowing anything much about the Norse Gods at the time, I began reading some of the mythology, starting with the Eddas, and my initial thought was that it might be Heimdall. The more I read, the less that seemed to fit, and I discarded the idea, although I did maintain a personal fondness for Heimdall.

As time went on I started to have strange dreams that would always feature a pair of ravens, and eventually I connected the feeling of presence, the dreams, and what I'd been reading and came to the conclusion that the deity I was sensing was probably Odin. There was a pervasive feeling with all of this that he wanted me to honor him, to connect to him, but since I was so new to Heathenry I was somewhat hesitant. So I decided to talk to some of my friends who had been Heathen for much longer and quickly found out that Odin had a very complicated reputation in the religion. He was seen as a God with many valuable qualities and powers, but also one that was ruthless and who put the greater good, as he defined it, ahead of all else.

When I told a good friend that I had been dreaming of getting a valknut[2] tattooed over my heart, she was concerned. Actually her reaction was to ask me if I knew that the valknut was known as the 'insert spear here' symbol among many modern Heathens, and was viewed as a sign of willingness to sacrifice one's self to Odin. I hadn't been aware of that and learning about the symbol's grimmer connotations as well as the reputation Odin had for not only bringing positive things like inspiration and wisdom but also being associated with madness gave me pause. I still felt a strong, almost overwhelming, pull towards him. It was frightening but also compelling and I found myself researching as much as I could about Odin.

What I learned was both alluring and off-putting, almost in equal measure. The mythology paints a picture of a deity who is driven to gain wisdom even at great personal cost, but whose ultimate goal seems to be delaying the end of our world. Who will trick people by using their own words against them, but will also appear to people he favors in times of great need to help them. Who gave many gifts to humanity, including life itself, but who is also known as Bölverkr [evil worker] and will find the loophole in any contract to his own advantage.

Ultimately, I read as much as could and learned everything I could about Odin, as well as trying to connect to the presence I felt around me. I never lost that caution with him, although that is probably a good thing, but I also never lost that feeling of allure either. I suppose for me Odin is like good mead, delicious and smooth but with a dangerous kick if you don't watch yourself.

End Notes

1. Specifically he accuses Odin of practicing seidhr, which is often associated with the stigma of 'umanliness', and of living in Samsey as a witch, and traveling among humans as a magic worker, things that in the context of Norse society carried connotations of being ergi. Ergi itself is a complicated topic that is probably best understood within its cultural context. I suggest this as a good online resource for a better understanding of the subject http://www.vikinganswerlady.com/gayvik.shtml

2. We will discuss the valknut as a symbol of Odin in the next chapter.

Chapter Three

Odin Outside Norse Culture

woden worhte weos wuldor, alwealda rume roderas; i.e. Woden construxit, creavit fana (idola), Deus omnipotens amplos ceolos
[Woden constructed the holy altars, all powerful god of the great heavens]
Codex Exon. 341, Grimm, 1888, page 159

Odin was a God of many names and that can make it difficult to know in some cases exactly when and where we are reading about Odin, particularly outside Norse culture. We know that he was a main God of the Germanic peoples, and we see him in Iceland, Norway, and Sweden, for example. We also know that he was honored in cultures that were influenced by these groups, such as the Orkney Islands which at one point were colonized by the Norse.

The name we may know him best by is Odin but there is also a great deal of material for at least two closely related Gods, Wodan and Woden, who come to us from the Germanic and Anglo-Saxon cultures. There is no consensus about whether these are definitely Odin by other names or different Gods that are closely related and very similar. All of their names share the same etymological root and meaning, and their descriptions and mythology are very similar. Some people feel that when Gods share such a clear root with each other, even when they diverge and belong to distinct cultures in later periods, that they remain connected as different aspects of each other or as the same being under different names. Other people feel that the cultural divergence creates new beings, new unique individuals, which may have a common source but are separate. It is up to the reader to decide which view is preferred.

Wodan – the German Odin

Many people are familiar with the Norse God Odin, but less well known is his German counterpart, Wodan, who is similar but not identical. Wodan (Old High German Woutan) although almost certainly derived from the same root as Odin has several distinct characteristics. Let us look at Wodan as we see him in the German material.

The name Wodan or Wotan comes from Woutan which is from the older Indo-European root wodenaz, meaning "raging, mad, inspired" (American Heritage Dictionary, n.d.). It is from this deity name through the Old English that English speakers get the word "Wednesday" – Woden's day – although this has been lost in German, replaced with Mittwoch (literally "middle week"). This root is also where the name Odin comes from.

Jakob Grimm, writing at the end of the 19th century, was firmly convinced that Wodan was the primary God of the Germans, comparing him to both Mercury and Jupiter (Grimm, 1888). Although, like Odin, Wodan is associated with war and battle he seems to have amore benevolent nature and is associated with the harvest and produce of the land as well as gifts and blessings. Wodan in this sense is referred to as a harvest God who would be prayed to in the fall for a good crop (Grimm, 1888). He was more a God of the common man in this view, a deity who would be petitioned and looked to for a family's security not only from physical dangers but also from hunger. He was a deity, in this view, of prosperity and abundance, whose blessing would ensure a household's success. As Grimm explains:*If we are to sum up in brief the attributes of this god, he is the all-pervading creative and formative power, who bestows shape and beauty on men and all things, from whom proceeds the gift of song and the management of war and victory, on whom at the same time depends the fertility of the soil, nay wishing, and all highest gifts and blessings.* (Grimm, 1888).

However Wodan also has a less benevolent side associated with the Wild Hunt. In the Germanic areas the Wild Hunt is often led by Wodan, Frau Hulde, or both together, and sometimes may be led by Frau Perchta or Frau Gauden [literally Mrs. Wodan] (Berk, & Spytma, 2002).The Wild Hunt travels in the air, and appears as a group of dark riders, led by a Huntsmen who may be headless, with a pack of fearsome hounds, accompanied by a horde of spirits who sometimes appear as the newly dead or battle dead (Jones, 2003). Often in folklore the Hunt was said to ride in late fall and winter, particularly during the twelve nights of Yule. Grimm tells us that in Germany it was believed the Hunt rode during the time from Christmas to Twelfth Night or whenever the storm winds blew (Grimm, 1888). Seeing the Hunt could be an ill-omen and the Hunt itself could kill or drive a person mad, but conversely in some areas it was believed that meeting the Hunt bravely and politely could earn a person great reward. Woden's connection to the Wild Hunt was pervasive and showed that he was a God who could bring both blessing or bane not only through his effect on the crops but by his direct contact via the Hunt.

The best protection from the Wild Hunt is avoiding them by not traveling at night, especially during Yule or other dangerous times. Shelter can also be sought at the first sound of hunting horn or hounds in the air. However, should those fail or not be possible and should you meet the Hunt, and do not feel like taking your chances with them, there is this charm from 14th-century Germany:

Woden's host and all his men
Who are bearing wheels and willow twigs
Broken on the wheel and hanged.
You must go away from here.
(Gundarsson, trans. Höfler; Berk, & Spytma, 2002).

In the end then when we look at the German Wodan we see a complex deity who is both a god of the abundance of the harvest and the fearsome leader of the Wild Hunt, a god of fertility and feeding the living, as well as of death and the dead. Ultimately we can say that he rewards those who show him respect and earn his favor, but punishes, even torments, those who offend or insult him. While in some ways he resembles his Norse counterpart he also has distinct features as well, which should be appreciated.

The Anglo-Saxon Woden

The second main culture that we see Odin, or at least a cognate of Odin, appearing in is the Anglo-Saxon. Here we find him under the name of Woden (in Old English) or Wodan (Old Saxon), with the same meaning as in the other cultures. Very few stories about him have survived.

As with the Norse Odin we see Woden as the head of the pantheon, although we have less clear evidence to go by. We do have archeological evidence showing Woden's presence in England through the Anglo-Saxon period as well as proof of his existence there and importance found in place names (Rowsell, 2012). What textual evidence we do have shows some clear parallels to the Norse Odin, for example Woden was seen as a God of magic, victory, and battle, and was connected to the Anglo-Saxon runes (Turville-Petre, 1964).

Anglo-Saxon sources connected Woden to the Roman Mercury, likely as a reflection of the interpretatio romana, but interestingly, some such as Ælfric of Eynsham, in the late 10th century tried to differentiate Woden from the Norse Odinn, possibly in an attempt to separate the God of the pagan Norse – enemies of the Christian Anglo-Saxons at that time – with the then euhemerized Woden who was often claimed as a royal ancestor of noble families (Rowsell, 2012). There is at least one notable difference between the Norse Odin and Anglo-Saxon Woden, which is in the imagery of Woden from Anglo-Saxon sources where he has both eyes (Kershaw, 2000). This may indicate an important difference between Odin and Woden, or may simply be incidental to the imagery we have; because of the lack of in-depth surviving mythology it is impossible to be certain.

It was common to see Anglo-Saxon kings tracing their ancestry to Woden, likely as a means of connecting royal houses to each other and of establishing equal footing with others making the same claims (Rowsell, 2012). Or basically, when the other noble houses claim descent from a God it is wise for your family to do so as well. Interestingly there was an established and ritualized pattern to the form of these claims which made it clear they were not meant to be interpreted literally but seen on a more symbolic level. When a person was reciting their lineage back to Woden, they would say that they were the tenth generation from him, placing exactly nine generations from Odin to them (Rowsell, 2012).

Although we have less evidence to work from it is generally accepted by scholars that Woden is related to the Norse Odin. What we do have points to some striking similarities particularly in the purviews of Woden and his strong connection to the nobility.

Odin in My Life

Although my main initial connection was to the Norse Odin I also developed a strong connection to the German Wodan over time. It's challenging to connect to a deity that doesn't have a lot of established mythology but I found a great deal of value in working on an experiential level to understand Wodan through meditation and dream-work. Being pushed to get out of a strictly book-oriented approach was definitely something I needed at that point in my life and it opened me up to mysticism in ways that have proved very useful since.

I found that I particularly connected to Wodan in his role with the Wild Hunt and with him came Frau Holle, and a deeper connection to the Hidden Folk. He also helped me move past some deep seated fears I was carrying with me and accept certain aspects of myself, by learning to relate to the Wilde Jagd, that I had previously staunchly rejected. In this way Wodan revealed layers of meaning and depth within my spiritual life that hadn't been there before, enriching something that I was perfectly content with beforehand.

I have found that this is often true of Wodan – or Odin by any name – that he will challenge us in unexpected ways, even ways that make us angry with him, but he will also lead us around to things that are great blessings without us ever realizing that he is doing so. He acts in ways that are obvious but also ways that are very subtle, and only later become clear. It was a hard lesson for me to learn that sometimes I do not get the answers of 'why' beforehand but have to trust and follow where he is leading. This isn't easy when the God in question is just as much associated with madness, frenzy, and betraying those he favors to the blade (so they will be brought to his hall) as he is with poetic inspiration, victory, and magic.

The sort of discernment Wodan teaches is valuable indeed.

Chapter Four

Symbols, Animals, and Items

"Who are the twain that on ten feet run?
three eyes they have, but only one tail.
All right guess now this riddle, Heithrek!"
Heithrek said: "Good is thy riddle, Gestumblindi,
and guessed it is: that is Odin riding on Sleipnir."
Heiðreks Gátur

As one might expect with a God as complicated and multi-layered as Odin, he has a variety of symbols, mythic places, beings, animals, and items associated with him. Each is symbolic in itself and also has meaning in connection to Odin, so in this chapter we will look at the main ones and the most salient information about them. By understanding the things associated with Odin we can gain a better and deeper understanding of Odin himself.

Valknut

One of the symbols that is most strongly associated with Odin in modern times is the Valknut, a symbol of three interlocking triangles. We see this symbol carved on a variety of items during the Heathen period, although its exact meaning in context is unclear. Hilda David Ellison theorized its connection to Odin by suggesting it related to his power:

For instance, beside the figure of Odin on his horse shown on several memorial stones there is a kind of knot depicted, called the valknut, related to the triskele. This is thought to symbolize the power of the god to bind and unbind, mentioned in the poems and elsewhere. Odin had the power to lay bonds upon the mind, so that men became helpless in battle, and he could also loosen the tensions of fear and strain by his gifts of battle-madness, intoxication, and inspiration. (Ellis-Davidson, 1964).

In modern Heathenry the symbol is possibly the main one associated explicitly with Odin, and is known in particular as a mark of dedication to him. I know many people who see wearing the valknut as a serious commitment to Odin, and those who choose to dedicate themselves to this ambiguous deity may choose to have the symbol tattooed onto their body.

Valhalla

The most well-known place associated with Odin was certainly his hall, named Valhalla, or 'Hall of the slain'. Many modern Heathens focus on going to Valhalla after death, as if Odin's hall was the Heathen equivalent of the Greek Elysian Fields, the reward, the good place that everyone should seek to get to, but that is not so. First of all Odin's hall is described in the *Prose Edda* as a place of slain warriors, who, for fun, battle each other all day and drink and feast all night (Young, 1964). The mead, literally, flows freely there and the party, and fighting, never ends but it's not a peacefully relaxing place. It is the gathering place of the Einherjar, the warriors who will fight for the Gods during Ragnarok. I tend to imagine it as something along the lines of a really rowdy biker bar. The mead is supplied by a goat named Heidrun, and is served to the Einherjar by the Valkyries (Simek, 1993). The feasting comes from the flesh of a boar named Saehrimnir, who is killed and renewed every day.

Valhalla is described as being a hall thatched in spears and shields, filled with armor for the einherjar. The goat that provides them with mead stands on the roof and eats leaves from Yggdrasil, the world tree. Valhalla is said to have 540 doors and is enormous on the inside, able to hold all the Einherjar and Valkyries (Simek, 1993).

Some people insist that the only way to get to Valhalla is to die in battle, and it is true that the *Prose Edda* says that the battle dead go there and that Odin sends the Valkyries to choose those worthy of Valhalla (Young, 1964). However, Freya was said to have her choice of half the battle dead for her hall, Folkvangr as well, meaning that a battle death did not guarantee entrance to Valhalla. And you don't have to die in battle to go to Valhalla as in some cases those who died by other means went there. In *Egil's Saga*, Egil says that both his sons have gone to Odin's hall, despite the fact that one drowned and one died of a fever; Egil himself, although dedicated to Odin does not expect to go to Valhalla, but rather says he sees Hel waiting for him (Egil's Saga, 1997). Our Troth volume 1 also notes that Sigurdr and Baldr, both killed by weapons, go to Helheim, while Sinfjotli goes to Valhalla after dying of poison (Gundurson, 2006).

Hlidskjalf

The name of Odin's throne or seat from which he can see the entire world. Odin is the one most known for sitting on this high seat but he is not the only one who does so in a story; Freyr also sits on Hlidskjalf at least once and ends up love sick over the giantess Gerd after seeing her from the throne's vantage point. It generally seems that Odin uses the seat to watch things going on through the worlds, as another means to gain knowledge and keep up with current events.

Runes

In a practical sense the runes are simply letters, a variety of alphabets found in the Norse influenced areas. There are several, but the ones that are most common today are probably the Anglo-Saxon, Younger Futhark, and Elder Futhark. Futhark being simply the first six letters in order of the alphabet, just as the alphabet represents the Latin letters 'a' and 'b' respectively.

In mythology we are told that Odin found the runes after hanging for 9 nights on Yggdrasil, without food or water, pierced by his own spear. Looking down he had a vision of the runes below him. Not only the ones we know, but many other sets which belonged to the Gods, Alfar [elves], dwarves, and giants. The runes were given to mankind in the story of the *Rigsthula*, which relates how one of the Aesir under the pseudonym of Rig came to Midgard and fathered three classes of people, giving the secret of the runes to the ruling class. Although myth would suggest Heimdall was the one who did this, there is much supposition that it was actually Odin who traveled under the guise of Rig (Simek, 1993). This makes a lot of sense given Odin's proclivity for wandering and his intimate knowledge of the runes.

Ravens

Huginn and Muninn are Odin's two ravens; their names translate to 'thought' and 'memory'. Every day the two fly throughout the worlds and return to tell Odin what they have seen on their travels. One of Odin's by-names is 'Hrafngud' [raven god] and his connection to these birds is an ancient one (Simek, 1993). Of the two, Odin says in *Griminsmal* that while he would not want to lose Huginn he fears more for Muninn, indicating perhaps that on a symbolic level he values memory more.

Wolves

Geri and Freki are the names of Odin's two wolves. Both of their names mean 'Greedy One' (Simek, 1993). Odin takes no sustenance except wine, according to myth, and gives all of his food instead to these two wolves.

Berserkers

A particular category of warriors that were associated with Odin were the berserkers [probably meaning 'bear shirts'], an elite warrior class who would go into a frenzy when fighting. Berserkers would bite their shields, foam at the mouth, and scream, working themselves into a trance-like state where they seemed impervious to pain. In the *Ynglinga Saga* they are described this way: "Odin's men went into battle without armor and were as wild as dogs or wolves. They bit their shields and were stronger than bears or bulls." (Simek, 1993). Although in later periods the berserkers were viewed with fear for their out of control aggression; it seems that originally their ability to channel Odin's divine inspirational fury was viewed positively, giving them the ability to become fearsome animals and heroes (Kershaw, 2000).

The Wild Hunt

The Wild Hunt is a group of spectral horsemen who ride the air at night, accompanied by hounds and horses, and led by a fearsome Huntsman (or in some cases Huntswoman). The Hunt is found in several areas of Western Europe as well as America and who exactly they are as well as who leads them can vary depending on where they are, so that in Wales they are known to be fairies led by the God Gwynn ap Nudd, while in Norse lands they are the souls of dead warriors, or the dead more generally, led by either Odin or Odin and a consort (Jones, 2003). In the Germanic areas the Hunt is often led by Odin under the name of Wodan, or sometimes Frau Hulda, or both together, and parts of England by Herne. There has been some suggestion that Herne is either Odin in disguise or else if Herne is a purely literary character that his later development into a deity was heavily influenced by Odin (Ford, 2001). The hunt in Germany is also sometimes led by Frau Perchta, or Frau Gauden [Mrs. Odin], who led groups of dead children or witches through the sky (Berk, & Spytma, 2002). In the areas where it is led by Odin it may be called Odensjakt [Odin's Hunt], Oensjaegeren [Odin's Hunters] or Odin's Army. Odin's connection to leading the Hunt goes back in writing at least several hundred years and speculatively in oral tradition to the 13th century (Lecouteux, 1999).

The Wild Hunt is known to ride out at certain times of year, especially during Lent, which is usually March and April, as well as around Midsummer and Midwinter (Grimm, 1883). Meeting the Hunt was usually seen as a bad thing and people would flee indoors or avoid going out when the Wild Hunt was known to be abroad, because of the danger it represented, but it could also bring blessings to people who were clever enough to earn them. For example, in stories like "Wod, the Wild Huntsman" the protagonist meeting the Hunt is rewarded with gifts of meat and gold for his cleverness. Conversely offending the Wild Hunt might mean the person earning a more gruesome reward, such as the corpse of his own child or a severed human limb, while other times the Hunt would turn on the individual and tear them to pieces (Berk, & Spytma, 2002; Grimm, 1883).

The beings who make up the Wild Hunt itself in Norse and Germanic lands are most often the dead, often the battle dead who still appear to bear the wounds that killed them. These ghostly troops also included animals, particularly hounds and sometimes wolves, and horses that may have as few as two or as many as eight legs (Kershaw, 2000). It's possible that these horsemen are the Einherjar, although they may also be other members of the Dead associated with Odin.

The Wild Hunt may also have had a living counterpart, a cult of masked youths who engaged in ecstatic practices to connect to Odin and the spirits of the ancestral dead, and held processions at certain times of year (Kershaw, 2000). The Wild Hunt, particularly in Germany, had associations with blessing the harvest (Lecouteux, 1999). We may perhaps suggest that at least in Germany Odin as Wodan and his Wild Hunt was at one point connected to cultic practices that may have had many layers of purpose, possibly both connecting to the dead and blessing the land.

Sleipnir

Sleipnir is the son of Loki, born when Loki was in the form of a giant mare. His father is Svadilfari, a stallion who belonged to a giant who was building a wall around Asgard to try to win Freya, the sun, and moon by completing it within a short period. Loki had encouraged the Gods to accept the giant's offer, a bet of sorts, with the belief that the giant would fail. However, when it was clear that the giant was going to win and finish on time, the Gods expected Loki to fix the problem and ensure the giant did not win the prizes he sought. The only way he could succeed at this was to take the form of a mare and lure the giant's stallion away, because without the huge horse the giant was unable to move the amount of stone needed to finish the wall. The result, some ten months later, was the eight legged horse Sleipnir who serves as Odin's steed.

Sleipnir's name means Slipper or Sliding One (Simek, 1993). He is able to travel freely between any of the nine worlds, and there has been some supposition that his eight legs may represent this, with one leg for each world and his body itself symbolizing his presence in the ninth. Another theory is that his gray color and eight legs are meant to be symbolic of the wind, while yet another suggests the eight legs represent the legs of pall bearers carrying a casket (Grundy, 1994).

In most stories Sleipnir only carries Odin, and we have images from the Heathen period of Odin riding this easily distinguished horse, although in one story Odin's son Hermod also rides him in order to travel to Helheim to ask for Baldur's release.

It is also best to remember that while he may be in the form of an eight-legged gray stallion, Sleipnir is actually the child of Loki and likely as sentient and intelligent as any of the other giants in animal form.

Gungnir

Odin's main and most well-known weapon is his spear Gungnir. The name means 'the swaying one' in Old Norse (Simek, 1993). Gungnir was made by the dwarves and brought to the gods by Loki, along with several other treasures. So profound was Odin's connection to the spear as a weapon that several of his names relate back to this weapon, including 'Gungnis Vafadr' [gungnir's shaker] and Geirs Drotinn [spear lord] (Simek, 1993). He is often depicted in images with his spear.

Draupnir

Another treasure of the Gods forged by the dwarves and obtained by Loki, Draupnir's name means 'Dripper' and it is said that every nine nights it drops eight new arm rings of the same weight. This symbolism of 9 and 8 is an interesting mirror of Sleipnir's eight legs and traveling the nine worlds.

According to the *Poetic Edda* Odin placed Draupnir with Baldr on his funeral pyre and by some accounts Baldur is now the owner of this treasure (Simek, 1993). Simek sees Draupnir as a type of temple ring or oath ring and sees Odin's ownership of it as symbolic, and he references other sources who view the arm-ring as a symbol of Odin's sovereignty.

Odroerir

The great mead of inspiration, brewed from the blood of the giant Kvasir by the dwarves who killed him. The name means 'one who stimulates to ecstasy' in Old Norse (Simek, 1993). In myth the mead was kept in three vats of lessening size. Odroerir was stolen from the giants who were guarding it by Odin, and was later viewed as something he possessed and could control the distribution of.

Yggdrasil

The world tree of Norse mythology is also closely connected to Odin. The name Yggdrasil means 'Yggr's horse' and Yggr is one of Odin's many by-names. The tree is an evergreen and by many accounts in the mythology is said to be an ash tree, although some suggest it may be a yew (Simek, 1993). There are several theories as to why the World Tree is called Odin's horse including the idea that the tree is somehow symbolic of a gallows, which Odin was connected to by several of his by-names, or that it was because he hung on the tree to find the runes.

Its roots drink from three wells in three of the worlds, one of which is a well of fate tended by the three Norns, deities who control the past, present, and future destinies of all things. The Aesir meet daily at this well, Urd's Well, to discuss important matters (Simek, 1993). The trees roots are gnawed on by a great serpent, or dragon, named Nidhoggr who also chews corpses and drinks blood in Helheim. The bark and leaves are eaten by four stags, and in the crown of the tree lives an eagle; a squirrel named Ratatosk runs back and forth between the eagle and Nidhoggr, carrying insults from one to the other, from the top of the tree to the roots and back up again.

Odin in My Life

Of all my personal stories about the Gods, I must admit this is probably one of the strangest.

The summer after I first started connecting to Odin I was feeling a strong urge to dedicate myself to him, but I was really hesitant to do so, largely because I was so new to Heathenry. I knew that within Heathenry there was a concept of dedication to deity, called 'fulltrui' but I also knew that it was generally something that developed slowly over time, like any good friendship, not something one threw one's self into. So despite the constant nagging feeling it was something I needed to do I kept rationalizing my way out of it. I was having dreams of ravens but it's fairly easy to ignore dreams during the day.

Then the squirrel showed up.

One day over the summer when I was alone in my house I looked out the sliding glass doors onto the deck and sitting on the railing looking back at me was a gray squirrel. As I watched, it turned its head and I could see that it was missing its right eye. After a moment – long enough for me to get a clear look at the missing eye – it turned and left. I thought it was curious, because you don't generally see small prey animals surviving missing an eye like that. I may live in the suburbs but there's a variety of dangers for an animal like a squirrel, from the natural ones like coyotes, fisher cats, and hawks to the human-made ones like cars. I was also curious about how the animal had survived whatever injury had caused the eye to be lost, if it was lost through trauma, or wondered if it had been born that way.

I didn't expect to see the squirrel again, but to my surprise I did. Regularly. And I began to notice a pattern; I only saw the squirrel when I was thinking about Odin, or worrying over whether I should or shouldn't dedicate to him. Once I was out on the deck contemplating my spirituality and the squirrel actually walked right up to within a few feet of me on the railing. I was on its blind side so it couldn't see me, and after a startled moment of staring at it, frozen, I made a noise so that it realized I was there and fled. I thought again how odd it was that an animal with that sort of issue had survived.

Seeing my little one-eyed friend became a regular thing over that summer, and I started to expect it to appear anytime I was in my house and thinking about Odin. And generally speaking it did.

Then I finally decided that rational or not I was going to take the plunge and formally oath myself to Odin. It was something of a leap of faith on my part, but at the time it felt like the right thing to do. I'd attended an oracular seidhr session and received a message that had confirmed the feelings I'd been getting for months, and that, combined with the ongoing dreams and feeling of presence, decided me. And once my mind was made up, I stopped seeing my one-eyed squirrel.

Chapter Five

Odin in the Modern World

Better ask for too little than offer too much,
like the gift should be the boon;
better not to send than to overspend.
Thus Odin graved ere the world began;
Then he rose from the deep, and came again.
Havamal (Bray, 1908).

The Odin of myth and history is a multifaceted God who can be seen in both a good and terrifying way. He inspires poets but he also brings madness and fury. He grants victory but he also claims heroes in battle, often when they think they have his favor. As much as we can know him from his place in history though we can also find him in the modern world, connected still to the roots of the old. As popular as he was in the pre-Christian Heathen period he may be even more popular among those who follow the many varieties of Norse religion today.

Two caveats should be mentioned now, before we get into discussing Odin in the modern world. Just as Odin himself is a God that has unpleasant features and stories – we shouldn't forget how Vali was conceived, no matter how uncomfortable the story may be – his worship today is also marred by things that a new follower or person interested in him should be aware of. Firstly, there is something of a fear of honoring Odin among some people, described in the book *Our Troth volume 1* as 'Odinphobia'. As much as some may love him beyond reason, others fear him for his associations with battle and madness, and his penchant in some stories for withdrawing his favor from people when they need it most, to bring them to his hall. There are those who call him an oath breaker, although whether he

51

actually breaks any oaths or merely slides around the letter of them may be a debatable point. The second, more significant issue, is that Odin's name and his worship have been co-opted in some contexts by people with very specific racist agendas. This is both deeply unfortunate and something that anyone venturing into studying Odin or honoring him in the modern world must be aware of. Not all followers of Odin or Heathen groups are racists or have racist subtexts but you need to be aware that some do, and that some of these groups twist Norse mythology and the Gods to justify their beliefs. Whatever your personal stance on the subject happens to be, it should be kept in mind that there is nothing in mythology that actually does support racism[1]; just the opposite in fact. We are told in the Eddas that Odin and his brothers created all men, and we see Odin, and several other Gods, mingling their blood with human family lines. We also know from history that the Vikings were quite willing to intermix with different populations as they moved into new areas, without any indication that they were concerned about purity of their tribal lines; children by foreign wives were still considered part of the dominant culture they were raised in (i.e. Norse).

That all said let's look at a few ways that Odin may be related to in a modern context, based on historic material, that may be innovative or new in different ways.

Odin as a God of Healing

When Odin is mentioned in conversation most people probably do not immediately think of him as a healing deity. God of battle, of the valiant dead, of poetry, of kings, of runes, even of magic or wisdom, but probably not healing. However, I have personally related to him this way for many years and often pray to him to heal illnesses and injuries. Admittedly this began as my own personal practice because it seemed natural to go to Odin for pretty much anything since I dedicated to him, but as it turns out there is some evidence that he may have been seen as such historically as well. So let's look at the historic evidence of Odin as a god of healing.

There are two examples of Odin being referred to or prayed to as a healing God; both appear in 10th-century manuscripts. One is the Anglo-Saxon *Nine Herbs Charm* which refers to Woden in relation to herbal healing, and the other is the Germanic second Merserburg Charm which refers to Wodan healing an injured horse.

The Nine Herbs Charm, excerpt:

> *A snake came crawling, it bit a man.*
> *Then Woden took nine glory-twigs,*
> *Smote the serpent so that it flew into nine parts.*
> *There apple brought this pass against poison,*
> *That she nevermore would enter her house*
> (Cameron, 1993)

The second Merserburg Charm:

> *Phol and Wodan were riding to the woods,*
> *and the foot of Balder's foal was sprained*
> *So Sinthgunt, Sunna's sister, conjured it.*
> *and Frija, Volla's sister, conjured it.*
> *and Wodan conjured it, as well he could:*
> *Like bone-sprain, so blood-sprain,*
> *so joint-sprain:*
> *Bone to bone, blood to blood,*
> *joints to joints, so may they be glued*
> (Fortson, 2004)

In the Nine Herbs Charm we see Odin invoked against poison in relation to a larger herbal magic charm. In the Merserburg Charm we see him invoked in conjunction with Sinthgunt (unknown outside of this reference but referred to as a sister of Sunna), and Frija (Frigga) to heal what could be a severe sprain or broken leg of a horse.

I tend to believe the similarity may reflect a pattern of healing charms found in both cultures which leads me to believe that the Merserburg Charm was likely to have been used as a healing chant over a certain type of injury. The two healing charms are enough for me to feel that he was likely to have been called on for healing, at least in certain areas and during a later period, and that, as they say, is good enough for me.

I have viewed Odin as a god of healing for many years and I pray to him in conjunction with other deities including Eir. I would say that for myself I have found that he is very effective in this capacity, but his help in this area is always at a cost in proportion to what is being asked for. When I am willing to pay that price he has literally preformed miracles[2]; when I am not willing to pay then the offer stays open, as it were.

Fulltrui - Dedication to a Deity in Heathenry

Within Heathenry you will see a wide range of approaches and beliefs, from those who don't believe in the Gods at all, to those who see them as archetypes, to those who believe the Gods exist as unique individual beings. In the same way you will see a range of approaches to how we relate to the Gods. At one end there are people who only acknowledge the Gods in ritual, while at the other are those who feel they have a special connection to one particular deity; most people likely fall into the middle of that spectrum. A person who feels especially close to one deity may refer to that deity as their fulltrui (for a God) or fulltrua (for a Goddess) which means, roughly, "trusted friend", and may refer to themselves as a man or woman of that deity – as in Odinssman or Odinswoman. Not everyone approves of the idea of such devotion to a deity and conversely many people mistakenly see it as necessary or required so I thought it would be helpful to discuss what it really is in a historic and modern context, especially as many people who honor Odin tend to be drawn to dedicating to him.

The following is, as always, my own opinions and views on the subject. As someone who considers Odin her fulltrui much of my viewpoint is shaped by my own experiences and understanding of the subject, although my choice to equate fulltrui and dedication may not be shared by everyone. I feel that having a "trusted friend" among the Gods requires a relationship of dedication to that deity; it's also the best verb I can find to describe the action of being fulltrui.

First off let's clear up one of the most common errors, that this idea is entirely modern and a holdover from monotheism. Although that argument is a common one against dedication, the idea of being dedicated to a God within a polytheistic Heathen context does have a historic basis. Many people try to argue against the entire idea of being fulltrui with a deity by attacking its authenticity as a Heathen practice, but there is enough evidence of people during the Heathen period who were dedicated to a specific deity to make the concept credible, although not common. We know that there were priests and priestesses dedicated to specific deities, such as the priestess of Frey who traveled the land with an effigy of the God in a wagon (Heinrichs, n.d.). and possibly the priest who served the shrine of Nerthus which Tacitus discusses in *Germania*. We also see more ordinary people, if such can be found in the Sagas, who were believed to be especially close friends of a certain God and would take that God's name as part of their own. We also know that it was not simply a matter of a person choosing to focus on one deity, but rather that the deity also seemed to be a "friend" to the person in return. In *Eyrbyggja Saga* Thorolfr Mosturskeggi who was known as a friend of Thor, a feeling that appears to be mutual as the story calls Thor the astvinr (beloved friend) of Thorolfr (Gundarsson, 2006). When making landfall in Iceland, Thorolfr trusted Thor to guide him to the best place to settle and build his new home by tossing his Thor pillars overboard and following where they landed. Thorgrim Freyrsgothi in *Gisla's Saga* was said to be so loved by Frey that the God would not allow snow to cover Thorgrim's grave. Within mythology even we can find examples of those particularly favored by a certain deity – Odin was known for this, although his favor might end in a bloody battle death – and we know that there were those who offered excessively to one deity to gain that favor, such as we see in the story of Ottar and Freya. So, from this we can see historic evidence of both priests and priestesses of one specific deity and also non-clergy who were considered close friends of a specific deity.

Now that we have established the precedent, let's look at modern fulltrui. The idea itself is fraught with confusion, both by people who aren't familiar with it and people who should be, and often this confusion is used to try to either dissuade or encourage the practice, which naturally creates more confusion. So I am going to try to discuss some of the most common things I hear and the reality of dedication.

Someone who is fulltrui with a deity is still a polytheist. Being close to one particular deity does not mean that other deities are not acknowledged or honored, or that the person is actually a monotheist. I am fulltrui with Odin and also regularly honor other Gods. Having a close connection with one deity in no way detracts from or lessens the honoring of other deities as well. Hand in hand with that, being fulltrui with a deity is not a way to cling to monotheism; I have never been a monotheist and have nothing of that to cling to, for one thing, and for another I have never met anyone who was dedicated to a deity who felt that their deity was the only or ultimate deity. I may be dedicated to Odin but I offer to many other Aesir and Vanir as well, and regularly acknowledge a combination of Gods. I pray for healing to Odin, but also to Eir. I honor Sunna with Sigdrifa's prayer each day. I offer to Frigga, Freya, Frey, Thor, Njordh and

Idunna during the year, and regularly offer to the landvaettir and my ancestors. The bulk of my practice centers on the alfar and huldufolk. Being fulltrui with one deity does not limit my honoring of others. Think of it as you would human friendship; even when you have one special close friend you still have at least a few other friends that you also spend time with and talk to.

Another common misconception is that people who are dedicated to a deity think they have some special direct connection to that deity that others don't and rely on that God or Goddess to make all their decisions. Someone who is fulltrui with a deity does not think they have a magic phone line to that deity or that the deity is involved in every tiny aspect of their lives, or at least I have only rarely encountered that mindset. There will always be some who believe that their God sends them messages in their cornflakes, or that they must consult their God about what color socks to wear, but the majority of people who are dedicated to a specific deity do not think that their deity cares about the minutiae of their life. There may be a sense or feeling of closer connection to that deity compared to other deities, there may be a belief in communication with that deity, especially by those like myself inclined to seidhrwork or who are particularly spiritual, but it is generally perceived as coming in dreams or in trances or altered states. Some people may indeed receive more direct communication more often, but they won't be the ones bragging about it to anyone who will listen or using it to try to prove that they are special. There is a difference between someone who is a mystic and someone who is being overly superstitious or seeking attention. I would never deny that modern people do encounter and communicate with the Gods, and people who focus more on a specific deity may experience this more often, but the idea that someone who is fulltrui with a deity has a direct line to that deity that other people don't is not accurate. We all have that connection to the

Gods we honor, whether we acknowledge it or not. Omens, of course, in a wider sense are believed in by many and would not fall into this context; for example I don't know anyone who wouldn't see thunder during a Thor blot as a positive sign.

Someone who is fulltrui may feel that they serve the deity they are dedicated to or they may not. I know people who simply accept that there is a special connection there and honor that with extra focus on that deity and more offerings, and I know others who serve their fulltrui in a capacity closer to that of a priest or priestess. As with human relationships no two are ever exactly the same, and that's a good thing. Some people formalize the relationship with an oath and others simply fall into it over time, without any official agreement. For those like me who do feel called to serve, the direction of that service may manifest as a feeling or intuition that certain things are wanted. I began studying seidhr for this reason and also began teaching rune classes from the same subtle feeling, and I got a valknut tattoo after being instructed to do so in a dream; divination can be used to verify or disprove these feelings. The person might also serve by doing things that they feel will honor their fulltrui or can be seen as a type of offering. I have ravens tattooed on my body as a voluntary offering to Odin, for example. In ancient times a person would have become a priest or priestess in a temple or shrine (as in Upsalla or Tacitus's account in *Germania*) or may have traveled with an effigy of the God, as in the story of Frey's priestess. In modern times this service takes a different form, although I do know one Freyaswoman who serves by maintaining a traveling shrine to Freya at various events.

Being fulltrui with a deity is not a requirement of Heathenry, nor is it necessarily the norm. The idea that all new Heathens need to find a patron deity to dedicate to is something that is increasingly common and totally superfluous. Modern Heathenry, as a religion, is not based on this idea at all, and in fact for a new Heathen such a focus could have a negative impact on building a feeling of connection with all the Gods in general. Dedication should be an organic process which occurs over time based in mutual responsiveness, not a quest to meet an imagined goal. Quite frankly, since deeper dedication to a deity can prove extremely challenging, I honestly don't know why anyone would seek it out. Ottar offered to Freya to gain a boon from her, and she turned him into a boar and rode him into Helheim to get what he sought. Odin's favored people tended to die in battle in the Sagas to earn their way into his hall as Einherjar. Everything has a cost balancing out the benefit.

Along with that last idea, although it does happen that a person comes to the religion through one God or Goddess, that singular connection should not get in the way of the wider connection nurtured by a polytheistic approach. Some people who are fulltrui with a deity mistakenly feel that all of their loyalty should be focused on that deity, and may even feel guilty for acknowledging or honoring others, but that idea, I think, is foreign to Heathenry. In other words, just because you may feel that Odin led you to find Heathenry doesn't mean you should only ever honor him. Honoring the Gods is intended to nurture reciprocity with them, and in order for this to create balance and blessing in our lives we must honor different deities who offer blessings in certain aspects of our life. Although having a fulltrui does mean going to that deity more often and for many different things it doesn't negate the wider benefits of having many Gods to offer to or call on.

Dedication is also not something to be taken lightly. One should never jump into dedication, both because oaths are a very serious matter and because it is, generally, a permanent relationship. If you dedicate to Odin you must be willing to give your life to him, or you should not do it. While occasionally a deity may release a person from dedication it's important to remember that in many ways it is not up to us, so we should never assume we can change our minds if we find out we don't like the experience. The Gods are real beings and what is offered, if accepted, is not ours to take back, any more than we can take back mead poured out on an altar. In the same way as Odin offered himself to himself on the Tree, I made myself an offering to Odin; not all offerings are accepted – mine was. It cannot be taken back, or undone, although like any friendship sometimes things naturally run there course and the relationship changes. Remember that the entire idea of fulltrui is that it goes both ways; we are friends to that God and that God is a friend to us. We have free will and can choose not to nurture that friendship, just as the deity may not accept our friendship, but once the bond is forged, particularly if oaths are involved, it cannot easily be broken.

Which leads us to the final point; dedicating to a deity is not a matter of deciding that you really like one particular God or Goddess. It also, I hope obviously, is not about wanting to impress or intimidate people. Many people seem to feel that if they really admire or relate to a specific deity then they should dedicate to that deity, but the reality is that dedication is in many ways a calling. Not only must we be willing to dedicate ourselves to that deity but the deity must want and accept our dedication. And sometimes, maybe most times, the deity who calls us will not be the one we expect or would have chosen ourselves. I am very fond of Heimdall and felt a special connection to who he is and what he represents, yet it was Odin who called me – not who I would have expected or chosen for myself. Being fulltrui with a deity is more than just really liking that God or Goddess; it's about feeling that the deity is responsive to you and being willing to repay that responsiveness.

Dedication is a modern concept rooted in past practices. It is something that can be very fulfilling but also very challenging, as reciprocity requires that as much be given as is received. It is a personal connection that exist between an individual and a deity, and in most ways it is significant only to the individual. It does not make you special or a better Heathen, just as not having a fulltrui isn't better or more genuine. Being fulltrui is about putting your trust in a deity, and having that deity respond as your astvinr, a beloved friend; it is about that special connection which is forged with time and commitment, rather than whim.

Connecting to Odin - A Basic Meditation

A good, basic way to begin connecting to any spirit or deity is to reach out to them through guided meditations and journeywork. I am including a simple guided meditation here for anyone to use to talk with Odin if they want to. Before doing this you would want to set the intention of meeting with him. It is also a very good idea to keep in mind that anything said in a meditation or journey has just as much weight and power as something said in the waking world, so I would advise caution in what you may say to him and how you say it. Choose your words carefully, remember that promises or oaths are binding, and that he is known as a God who can be tricky.

Sit comfortably where you won't be disturbed. Take several slow, deep breaths. Close your eyes. See yourself walking down a sunlit path through the woods. The trees are heavy around you, the sun filtering in through the leaves. As you walk the trees slowly begin to thin. You realize there is a clearing ahead and you move towards it. The trees open up and you step into an open space, surrounded by a circle of trees. The air is still and silent, as if the world was holding its breath.

Into the stillness steps a figure – it is Odin. Look at the figure: how does he appear to you? What is he wearing? How does the energy around him feel? Stepping towards you he tells you his name and gives you a message. If you want to ask him any questions, now is your chance, otherwise you can just listen to whatever he has to say to you. Take as long as you need, and thank him when you feel your time is done. When Odin leaves turn and go back down the path.

Go back through the tunnel of trees. The trees around you begin to grow denser, thicker as you walk. The light gets darker. Take several deep breathes. Feel yourself fully back in your body. Wiggle your fingers and toes, stretch. Open your eyes when you are ready.

Offerings to Odin

One way to help build a relationship with Odin, if you are interested in doing so, is by offering to him. This is something we see as a key feature in Norse religion which emphasized the importance of reciprocity. We give to the Gods and they give to us and we give to them, endlessly.

In mythology it is said that Odin does not eat solid food but only drinks, specifically according to the *Gylfiganning* he drinks wine and gives any food to his wolves. Despite this I know people who do offer him food, particularly things like salmon, although for myself I see it as an offering that he likely accepts and then passes on. It is more common to see people giving him alcoholic beverages, including mead, aquavit, and the aforementioned wine. I have also personally offered poetry and writing to him, sometimes just by creating it and dedicating it in his name and sometimes by burning the only copy of a written work that I have.

When doing rune work I will offer to him and ask for guidance or help understanding the runes. In other situations I may offer to him with a purpose or I may simply offer to him for the sake of creating that reciprocal relationship.

If you feel motivated to offer to Odin you could leave a cup out in his name on your sacred space or altar, or you could dedicate the same to him and pour it out on the ground. You might decide to put something out to feed ravens if you have any in your area (be warned they prefer meat) or you might offer him the result of your skill, including poetry. Exactly how you decide to create this connect will vary depending on your own spirituality and religious approach, but with Odin at least I have found that the effort itself does count for something.

Odin in My Life – the Story of my Odin Staff

One of the physical objects that I would describe as my most precious possession is an ash staff hand-carved with images relating to Odin. The staff was made by the amazing Paul Borda, of Dryad Design, and is something I use in my seidhr work among other things. And yes the staff has a name, but it often is referred to simply as the Odin Staff, and it has gained its own reputation among my friends for personality. I could tell you stories about how it seems to look at people, in a way that unnerves many, or about how it doesn't seem to like my husband who mysteriously ends up tripping over it whenever he is near it, even when the tripping is inexplicable. But I think instead I will tell you the story of how I came to have the Odin Staff and why I believe that it is okay to ask the Gods for help when we feel they are asking us for something.

About a year before, I had begun thinking of getting a staff to use with seidhr work. The seidhrkona in *Eric the Red's Saga* used a staff and several modern practitioners have mentioned using one; I found the idea intriguing and was contemplating working it into my own practice. I have a couple of staves already, but none of them felt right for use in seidhr so I was tentatively thinking of making my own, a daunting prospect given my past failures in that area.

I'd been debating back and forth with myself for several months actually about using or not using a staff and making one or not and hadn't made any firm decisions, when in late January of that year I saw a link to an e-bay listing for a staff by Paul Borda. I can't accurately describe the intense and immediate feeling that this staff was meant to be mine. It was overwhelming. I had never been on e-bay before and I had an ingrained mistrust of any online auction sites but I followed the link like Alice diving down the rabbit hole. The staff was beautiful, and it was perfect. Made of ash wood it was intricately carved with an image of Odin, his two ravens, his two wolves, Sleipnir, and the rune ansuz. Odin was holding a horn (I imagined of mead) in one hand, and his spear Gungnir in his other hand. The detail was stunning and I was in love. The price, however, was prohibitive, so I sadly told myself it was not to be.

The auction ran for a week. Every day I found myself obsessively thinking about the staff in a way that was not normal. I couldn't get it out of my mind and I found myself fighting the temptation to place a minimal bid on it, even though I had bills to pay. Finally I started to wonder if this was all me or if some of this was rooted in Odin wanting me to have the staff; I realize how that sounds but at this point I could not explain why I was so obsessed with it. The more I thought that it was something he wanted me to have, the more sure I became that it was so, but the rational part of my mind kept interjecting that it could just be my own desire. Why, after all, would a deity care what kind of a staff I used, even if I was dedicated to him and it was for work I do because of him? I am fond of beautiful things, and it could just as easily have been my own desire talking. Finally I thought of some advice I'd been given years ago by another seidhrworker and Odinswoman that I very much respect. She told me that sometimes the Gods may want us to do certain things for them, and in those cases there is nothing wrong in asking for their help in getting what we need to accomplish what's being asked of us.

I thought long and hard about this, and about whether there was any possible way I could get the needed money. My family had just filed our tax return and I knew we had some money coming back; this is the only real spending money of any quantity that I have during the year and I already had a list of books and other items that I was planning to get. But I also knew that it had always taken at least two weeks for the tax refund to show up in our bank account and that would be long after this auction closed. It seemed impossible for me to work this out on my own in any way.

That Wednesday I stood before my altar, lit a candle, and made a small offering. I asked Odin, if it really was true that I was meant to have this staff or that he wanted me to have it for my seidhr work, that he help me to have the money in time. In exchange I said that I would spend every penny that I had for spending money if it came to that, to try to get the staff, and forego all the other items I had wanted to get.

I walked away feeling like it was out of my hands now, one way or another.

The next day when I checked my bank account (to balance my checkbook) the tax return money had been direct deposited. A record three days after filing the return. It freaked me right out. I actually went back and triple checked it to be sure it was really there. And then I remembered my end of the agreement and went up and placed a bid on the staff, which I won two days later when the auction closed.

Even now telling the story it seems unreal, but that is exactly what happened, the way that it happened. And I have had the staff ever since.

The biggest lesson I got out of this was that it really is okay to ask the gods for help when we feel that they want us to do something. If they really want it then they will help with it (obviously how to tell what they want is an entirely different topic). In the past when I felt that something was wanted of me I always took it as a personal challenge. It is hard for me to ask for help, even divine help, because I always rely on myself to get things done or to work things out, so this was probably a lesson I needed to learn.

End Notes

1. Racism isn't supported in the lore, however, classism arguably is. We see this as something that the gods

establish after one of the Aesir comes to earth disguised as Rig and fathers three different classes of men: thralls, freemen, and nobles. However, just because this loose class system is established in the mythology does not mean that it is morally supportable today, any more than human sacrifice is, which is another thing we see in the pre-Christian Heathen period.

2. My second child was born with several chronic medical issues. One of these was a congenital immune deficiency disorder. Effectively she was born missing the part of her immune system that protects mucous membranes, making her prone to any and all infections of those areas. When she was a toddler, after years of serious repeated infections and near-hospitalization over things like the flu, in desperation, I went to Odin. I offered to him and prayed to him. And the next time she had bloodwork done her body had begun inexplicably producing the immunoglobins that her body had previously lacked. This was so baffling to her doctors that they re-tested her, and then proclaimed that somehow she had been previously misdiagnosed because disorders like hers simply do not spontaneously cure themselves – or so I was told.

So I credit him with a miracle.

However, there is a reason I didn't and won't go to him for help with her other health issues. Some costs are too high to pay.

Chapter Six

Magic with Odin

Songs and runes then can do very great things. They are able to kill and bring to life, as well as prevent from dying; to heal or make sick, bind up wounds, stanch blood, alleviate pain, and lull to sleep; quench fire, allay the sea-storm, bring rain and hail; to burst bonds, undo chains and bolts, open mountains or close them up, and unlock treasures; to forward or delay a birth; to make weapons strong of soft, dull the edge of a sword; loop up knots, loose the bark off a tree , spoil a crop; call up evil spirits and lay them, to bind thieves... The Rûnatal, Sæm. 28-30, specifies eighteen effects of runes.
Grimm, Teutonic Mythology

Runes

One of the things most strongly associated with Odin are the runes, as discussed previously. The runes serve many functions in the old Norse culture and mythology, and just as many today. They are, obviously, an alphabet but also have magical and divinatory uses. What we know about them historically is a blend of actual history and myth.

Rune magic is a controversial topic in modern Heathenry, often accused of being New age-y or not genuinely Heathen, but it is a topic that we have a good amount of evidence for. Runes are mentioned in Norse and Germanic myth in connection to magic fairly often and fairly explicitly. The greatest challenge in a modern setting is that not all the references are easily interpreted and some of the runes referenced are not clearly identifiable with the named runes we know today. As Grimm says in his Teutonic Mythology:

The olden time divided runes into many classes, and if the full

import of their names were intelligible to us, we might take in at one view all that was effected by magic spells.
(Grimm, 1888)

We do know that to use rune magic the rune or a series of runes was usually carved or painted on something. Grimm tells us, "They were painted, scratched or carved, commonly on stone or wood, 'run-stones, runstaves'; reeds served the same purpose." (Grimm, 1888). In *Egil's Saga* Egil saves himself from a poisoned drink when he carves a rune on a drinking cup and chants over it; the cup bursts, spilling the poison on the ground. Sigdrifamal lists a series of runes and their uses, including carving Tiwaz twice on the hilt of a weapon for victory:

Sig-runes thou must know, if victory (sigr) thou wilt have,
and on thy sword's hilt grave them;
some on the chapes,
some on the guard,
and twice the name of Týr.
(Sigdrifamal)

The story also goes on to discuss "Beer" runes to carve on a drinking horn and the backs of your hands, with Nauthiz scratched on the fingernails, to keep other's from telling your secrets. "Help" runes are drawn on the palms of the hands of a midwife or her assistant to aid a mother in childbirth, and prayers to the disir are recommended. "Sea" runes must be carved on the prow and helm of a ship and burned into the oars for safety at sea. "Branch" runes are used, drawn on bark and leaf, to aid in healing. "Speech" runes are used for eloquence and "Thought" runes for wisdom.

The challenge, obviously, is working out which rune is a "beer" rune and so on. Different modern authors and practitioners will have differing opinions on which should be what, and it's important to keep in mind that it is all educated guess and experimentation. The "Sea" rune that works for me may not be the "Sea" rune that another person uses, and that is natural; certainly there was variation a thousand years ago as well.

In modern times runes are fairly well established as a means of divination, but are often criticized in Heathenry for not being historically used for that purpose. The truth is that we know the ancient pagan Norse and Germans used a system of lots for divination, but we don't know with certainty that the marks on the lots where runes, nor what each rune may have been interpreted to mean. We do, however, know that runes were used for magical purposes so it's not completely unrealistic to believe that the runes used so extensively in magic might also have been used as the marks on lots.

The *Havamal* says:

Hidden Runes shalt thou seek and interpreted signs,
many symbols of might and power,

Which at least hints at the possible use of runes for divination. Tacitus tells us:

For auspices and the casting of lots they have the highest possible regard. Their procedure in casting lots is uniform. They break off a branch of a fruit-tree and slice it into strips; they distinguish these by certain runes and throw them, as random chance will have it, on to a white cloth. Then the priest of the State if the consultation is a public one, the father of the family if it is private, after a prayer to the gods and an intent gaze heavenward, picks up three, one at a time, and reads their meaning from the runes scored on them. If the lots forbid an enterprise, there can be no further consultation that day; if they allow it, further confirmation by auspices is required. Tacitus, *Germania*

From this we can gather that the casting of lots was considered an important method to obtain answers to questions, especially those of ritual or communal importance. We also see that in Germania wood from a fruit tree was used and the runes were prepared fresh before each use. The exact ritual described involves throwing all the runes onto a white cloth and then looking up and blindly choosing three to answer the question asked.

In a modern setting runes are certainly used and generally the meanings, at least for those with a more reconstructionist bent are based on the old rune poems. These poems which come from Iceland, Norway, and Anglo-Saxon England can be found in several places today, including Diana Paxson's book *Taking Up the Runes*, and while they were likely originally a mnemonic device for learning the alphabet (or futhark as it were) offer insight into things associated with each runic symbol. These associations can be expanded into meanings that can be associated with the rune for use in divination.

There are many good books on the market today that offer ideas and share the author's insight into possible divinatory meanings of each rune. I tend to recommend Diana Paxson's book *Taking Up the Runes* because it includes references and quotes from many other well-known authors as well as all of the original rune poems. Other popular choices are books written by Edred Thorsson (also known and published under the name Stephen Flowers), Freya Aswynn, Stephen Plowright, Kveldulf Gundarsson, and R.I. Best.

Seidhr

In 2006 or so when I started honoring the Norse Gods and Odin came calling, I became aware of the Norse practice of seidhr. We know from the available material that seidhr was something of an outsiders' practice, often equated in later material to witchcraft, and that men who practiced it were seen as unmanly. As with many such practices there is some division of the 'good' and 'bad', or positive and destructive practices into two different categories with people who were generally seen as positive being called spae workers while those with darker reputations were known as seidhr workers. The word spae means to prophesy and is related to the Old High German word 'spahi' meaning 'skillful' or 'wise' while the word seidhr is harder to define (Harper, 2017). Seidhr is often translated as witchcraft, although the word itself in Old Norse likely means 'spell, magic, enchantment' (Ellis-Davidson, 1973; Hyllested, 2010).

Seidhr and Spae have several similarities but also a few key differences, beyond reputation. One difference between them is the actual means of oracular work, as Simpson explains here, "... *seiðr could give the worker knowledge of the future, but rather than directly perceiving ørlög or fate, as a spá-kona or völva would, the seið-practitioner summoned spirits to communicate the knowledge of the future.*" (Simpson, J., 1973, p 183). In this way then a seidhr worker, one who works enchantments, is also a summoner of spirits, while a spea-worker, a wise woman who prophecies, sees the future directly. How exactly that is done particularly in modern terms may vary, but often involves the person engaging in some form of trance work.

There is evidence, such as the story of the Spaekona in *Eric the Red's Saga*, that people who practiced spae may have traveled from village to village as guests to foretell the community's fate. These people were respected for their abilities, although this fell out of favor in the Christian period.

According to *Ynglinga Saga* seidhrworkers were said to be able to control the weather by stilling the ocean or turning the wind, could put out fires, shapeshift by sending their spirit out in the form of an animal, could tell the future, could speak to the dead (a practice called utiseta or out-sitting) and could bring death, ill luck and illness, or life, good luck and health. The *Voluspa* mentions the seidhr worker's ability to influence the minds of other people and to use magic charms.

As I mentioned, seidhr had something of a bad reputation while spá or spae (interestingly spae is actually the Scottish version of the word) was viewed more benevolently. In terms of my own practice I do both but I have a bad habit of using the term spae for all oracular work even that which should technically be considered seidhr. Secondly both seidhr and spae involve practices that can be seen as manipulative of other people to various degrees. Yes, I actually use these methods; this isn't just academic discussion for me. I have spent over a decade – nearly two at this point – learning and practicing these things. I truly believe in them, and I really do them.

Any type of seidhr work, to me, involves some level of trance work and so needs to be done carefully and with protection. That may mean different things for different people and groups; to me it means warding the space when doing deeper work, especially oracular work, and having allies to watch my back. I am dedicated to Odin, who knows seidhr work, and I have a shrine to Freya, who they say was the first to teach seidhr to the Aesir. Before any planned working I offer to them both. I offer to my ancestors and to other particular spirits I work with when doing this type of work. For less intense daily work I trust to my personal wards and protection. If you don't know what that is or how to do it then you aren't ready to be doing any of this type of trance work. There are several good books on the market that can help with the basics, including *Trance-Portation* by Diana Paxson as well as some good internet resources[2] that also explain the basics and history of the practices.

I generally do things like weather work and shapeshifting when I am alone; it was common in traditional seidhr for the person working to withdraw to a quiet place alone and lay or sit with their head covered. In seidhr work this is called going under the cloak and was also used by skalds (poets); it is a type of meditation that can be used for a variety of purposes from spellcasting, spirit journeying, to contacting spirits and receiving prophecies and poetic inspiration. I have found that even putting my hands over my eyes is effective for entering a trance. Influencing the weather is not my forte, although I've had success with it; it takes a lot of energy and concentration and is usually done in a lighter trance. It involves, for me, going to where I want the change to manifest and then visualizing that change for as long as I can. It is a very tiring thing to do and I have only ever focused on very slight changes in localized areas. Calling storms is a seidhr practice that I have never done, although I have diverted the damage of a storm around my home. Shapeshifting can occur in any level of awareness, but I find I use it most often when my spirit is journeying outside my body, particularly when traveling in the Otherworld (hedgewitches call this "crossing the Hedge"). Such traveling, at least in human shape, seems to be common in modern seidhr, especially oracular work as many groups use a method where they journey to the gates of Hel or to the Well of Wyrd to answer questions. I haven't seen similar accounts in the lore, except in the case of one story where a man sent his spirit in the form of a bear to fight against some other men – the bear disappeared when the man was awakened from his trance.

When alone or with my own group I tend to use this traveling method to find answers. Now my personal preference for a public oracular method is different, based on what I have reconstructed from the story of the spae worker in *Eric the Red's Saga*. Although I base my practices off of a reconstruction of those from *Eric the Red's Saga* it would be more accurate to say that what I am doing is seidhr rather than spae because I am calling spirits to me, rather than going to them, or using another method to foresee anything.

I sit in a seat before the gathered people, with my face covered[1], and in my mind I recite a chant I have written to call any goodly inclined, helpful spirits to me to answer the questions that will be asked. This involves going into a deeper trance and after the session I will not remember anything that was said, by myself or others, although so far the results have been very good. I do not personally use drumming, although I can work and have worked with someone using drumming; it's just not something that I need. I am contemplating adding the use of a staff, both to hold and to tap on the floor, so that might be the next experiment. Most of what I do at this point is the result of years of trial and error learning and it is still evolving as I learn new methods.

Another seidhr practice is called sjonhverfing, or "deceiving of the sight". This involves making others see or perceive what you want them to instead of what is really there. An example of this type of seidhr magic is seen in *Eyrbyggja Saga* where a seidhr worker saves a man who is being chased by making the men chasing him see only a household object (a staff if I remember correctly) where the man is sitting. I have been doing this type of magic for far longer than any of the skills listed under the auspices of seidhr, and of all the practices I think this one is the most directly similar between the Irish and Norse. You simply focus on the other person or people seeing what you want them to see, and act as if you are fully confident that they see it. The real trick for me is to pay attention and only do it when I want to, because it's very inconvenient to accidently influence things. And probably irresponsible, but nobody is perfect, and like anything else getting control of this is a matter of practice and time.

A final well-known seidhr practice is utiseta, or sitting out. Utiseta is done to contact the spirits of the dead, by sitting out on a grave or mound wrapped in a cloak. Utiseta in the lore could be very dangerous but could also offer many rewards, especially through new knowledge and prophecy, which the Norse believed could be given by the dead. I have used utiseta with the dead in a cemetery only once; generally I use it to contact the land vaettir and alfar, particularly the drokkalfar or Mound Elves. It works perfectly well for that, and I've had a lot of success with utiseta as I do it.

Odin in My Life

I did not officially discover Odin until I was in my twenties, but I found the elder futhark runes as a young teenager. I'd like to say I had some noble purpose in learning them, or that I wanted to incorporate them into my paganism even back then, but the truth is far more pragmatic. I was 13 and a freshman in high school and thought writing in runes would be a great way for my friends and I to pass notes in class without worrying about getting caught. I taught myself to read and write them fluently and used them regularly. I knew, of course, that the runes had esoteric meanings and uses but because they didn't interest me at that age the awareness was a secondary thing that was easily put to the back of my mind.

A decade later when I started learning about Heathenry and found the deeper layers and meanings of the runes it was something of an epiphany. This system of writing that I'd been using for so many years suddenly opened up into a whole new thing for me. Since I already knew the symbols and what English letters they represented I picked up the esoteric meanings quickly and found that I really liked using the runes for both divination and magic. In divination I find that they are much more blunt and to the point than other methods I know, especially tarot, but they can also be equally opaque when they don't want to answer something. In magic they are effective on their own and can also be combined into bindrunes. I love this versatility.

Like so many magical practices the runes are one of those things that seem very simple on the surface and yet also have an endless depth to them. No matter how much I think I have learned about them, I am constantly realizing there is more to know. I have found that working with the runes in any capacity has deepened my knowledge and appreciation of Odin.

End Notes

1. most modern seidhr workers that I know of use a veil to cover their face during oracular work. I use a bear skin, with the face covering my own, because that's how I was told to do it. I don't argue with the People who have my back. By a wyrd coincidence the bear was given to me by a family member shortly after I was told I needed one, after it had spent many years as a rug; since acquiring it I made some offerings to its spirit and we are all copacetic now

2. further reading on historic and modern seidhr found online:
    http://www.vikinganswerlady.com/seidhr.shtml
    http://www.freyja.org/seidr.htm
    http://www.hrafnar.org/seidh.html
    http://www.sunnyway.com/fenvala/he_seidh.html
    http://www.boudicca.de/seidhr-e.htm

Chapter Seven

Prayers and Poetry

Odin is well known as a God of poets and poetry. I have found that as I honor him I have often been inspired to write for him, creating prayers and poetry in his honor. I think that this is a natural result of connecting to a deity whose nature is so strongly tied to the concept of inspiration. It was Odin who gained the mead of poetry and who shares it with those who he chooses, granting inspiration in creative arts especially those that focus on the clever use of words. During the Viking period we often see poets starting their work by claiming they have Odin's mead, and he was indisputably the chief patron of poets (Gundarsson, 2006). In the modern era this can still be an important aspect of this multifaceted God.

In this chapter I am going to include a variety of material that I have written for Odin, under both that name and some of his by-names. I also encourage people reading this to try writing their own prayers and poems. I realize some people find this idea intimidating, but I think there's a lot of value in using words we've put together ourselves, and in reaching out to a deity like Odin to help find those words. When I write for him sometimes the words just come on their own but other times I will reach out to him and ask for his help. I might light a small candle or make a small offering before I start to write.

Prayer to Odin for Writing

Grant me,
winner of Odrerir,
the poet's power
Let words be my weapons,
sharp, strong, and well aimed,
May my meaning be clear

May my message be persuasive,
May my methods be enchanting,
Odin, grant me inspiration

Prayer for Wisdom

Harbard, Wise Ferryman,
Help me learn patience
Help me learn to answer well
Help me find my wisdom
Graybeard, May it be so

Prayer for Abundance

Oski, Wish-giver, Will-worker,
I seek security and safety
I want my income to be sound
I am open to your guidance and gifts
May I find the blessings I seek
May my hard work be worthwhile
May my effort be rewarded
With abundance and prosperity

Invocation to Odin

Odin, Wanderer, Wise one,
I call to you
Hanged one, Hidden one, High one,
I call to you
Yule father, All father, Victory father
I call to you
Mighty God, I invoke you
Ancient One, I offer to you
Wand-bearer, I honor you

Prayer for Travel

Odin, wandering God

May my way be clear before me
Thor, God of might and main
May your hammer ward my way
Tyr great God and guiding star,
May I travel timely along my way
Safely I go forth,
Safely I shall return
By my will, it is so

Mead-Fire - A Poem

I drink the cup he offers
the horn-rim cold against my lips,
sweet honey taste in my mouth,
a single swallow spreads
down my throat
into my blood, my brain-
images burst behind my eyes,
words blossom fire bright in my mind
burn like ice into my memory,
Tumbling intensely through me
the swirling sensations barely
at the edge of what I can bear
as my fingers itch to find a pen,
for I know there will be no relief
until I free this vision from its fleshy prison,
release it into the world
like a child struggling to be born
only fully alive when it is separated.
And I know as well that despite the pain
I would drink again from that horn,
drink down the divine inspiration
in one swift swallow...
That moment is worth any madness,
any cost I might be called to pay.

Consumed

How you frighten me
so grim, so terrible
I want to run from your gaze
your eye, fixed on me,
sees too clearly for comfort
dissects me until I cry out –
not knowing what draws your stare
what am I to you, Father of Slaughter?

How you fascinate me
so great, so ruthless,
I want to rush to your side
to belong, to give in to you,
to let myself be seduced
consumed by your power –
not caring what will come of it
what am I to you, Allfather?

How you torment me
so implacable
I struggle against my feelings
opposing myself at every turn
I am no willing sacrifice
I do not want to give in to you –
not knowing where you want to lead me
what am I to you, Terrible One?

How you entice me
so unrelenting
I'm drawn like a moth to a flame,
unable to resist the fire
which I know will be my doom
the closer you feel, the more I pull back –

not capable of escaping your hold
What am I to you, Sleipnir's Rider?

How you consume me,
so inescapable
I feel overwhelmed by your presence,
feel trapped, feel wanted,
feel fated, feel lost, feel taken
by force, by something I can't resist –
not that I'm sure I want to
What am I to you, Odin?

Wanderer

I am a wanderer in the world
Shadow of a distant dream
Rootless and boundless,
I'm exactly what I seem

Thought and Memory's master
Every poet's inspiring friend
My hall will be many soldiers'
Destination in the end

I am sacrifice and strength
Ever in strife's company
Walking the line between
Madness and ecstasy

I grant wisdom and vision
Only to those willing to pay
The high price I ask of all
who would follow me on my way

I am fury and passion

To those who call my name
Many illusions disguise me
I change yet am the same

Hunter, sage and seeker
Both loved and often feared
I am active where I'm needed
I know all the worlds' wyrd

I am honor and doom
For those who to me have sworn
Challenge, testing and hardship
For those who drink from my horn

Wish-granter and victory giver
Powerful gifts – mine to bestow
Shaman, magician, and traveler
I go wherever I must go

I am a wanderer in the world
Lord, beggar, and ferryman
The end is ever coming
And I've much to do before then....

Storm

Tonight the darkness holds the land
And living things hide safe within –
I stand out in the wind and rain
While storm tossed clouds seethe overhead
And lightning burns across the sky
Thunder crashing like ocean waves
Breaking hard on an unseen shore
The Lord of Storms rides out tonight
His horse running on the wild wind

Cloak tearing at the rain soaked air
His eyes flashing bright as lightning
I stand and watch him rushing by
Wind and rain whipping through my soul
Then I'm left alone in the dark
As the echoing hoof beats fade
Waiting for one more flash of light
Waiting for the returning storm

Marked

I dream of raven wings,
of the sound of hoofbeats
echoing through the dark,
a shadow swooping down
leaving me no escape,
I turn to face a spear
pointed straight at my heart
and prepare for my fate.
The blade cuts into flesh
but does not spill heart-blood –
not today, no, not yet –
satisfied now to carve
a mark through skin and pain
down to my very soul,
and whirl away again
to leave me standing there
anticipating the
final, fatal thrust that
I know now awaits me

Conclusion

Every day the Gods meet at the well of Urd, a well kept by the Norns where the fate of all things is set, near the roots of the World Tree. Every day Odin's raven Huginn and Muninn fly out, gather information, and return to regale him with news of the world. And every day Odin seeks just a little bit more wisdom to stave off the inevitable Ragnarok. These things were true in the mythology and they remain true today, for those who still believe that the Norse Gods exist and walk in the world. Of course today you may not find Odin riding the street of a city in a helm and armor, but you might run across him as a one-eyed stranger, clad in worn blue and black clothes, riding the bus with you. It's an odd thought perhaps, but Odin is the wanderer, and he wanders still.

If you seek a God of wisdom, of poetry, of victory, if you seek a God of magic, of power, and of prophecy then you may find that Odin is what you are looking for. Or you may find that it's Odin who is looking for you. He does that, after all, seeking out those who add valuable skills he needs in his fight both now in staving off the Gods' fate and down the road in fighting the final battle. You may find that there are many reasons to honor him and come to value the many good gifts he gives.

But don't forget the other side of that coin, that the God of inspiration is also the God of madness and that the God of victory is also the God of the battle dead. Everything has a cost and the better the gift the higher the price.

Appendix A: Modern Media

There is a wide array of modern material featuring Odin including music and video games. I can really only touch on a small selection here, and I'm trying to stick to ones that either present the Norse Gods in a positive light or at least a fairly neutral one. Please keep in mind though that this is only a sample of some of the different media that you may find Odin depicted in today.

Fiction that incudes Odin:

Odd and the Frost Giants by Neil Gaiman
American Gods by Neil Gaiman
Brisingamen by Diana Paxson
Runemarks by Joanne Harris
The Dresden Files by Jim Butcher
The Iron Druid series by Kevin Hearne
The Magnus Chase and the Gods of Asgard series by Rick Riordan

The Thor comics in the Marvel Universe, as well as the related movies.

Several different anime series including High School DxD and Matantei Loki Ragnarok feature the Norse Gods.

The Norse gods, including Odin make appearances on the TV show *Supernatural*, and the TV series *the Almighty Johnsons* is about the Norse Gods reincarnated in modern New Zealand.

Bibliography

Adalsteinsson, J., (1999). Under the Cloak: a Pagan Ritual Turning Point in the Conversion of Iceland

—(1998). A Piece of Horse Liver: Myth, Ritual and Folklore in Old Icelandic Sources

American Heritage Dictionary (n.d.) https://www.ahdictionary.com/word/indoeurop.html

Bauschatz, P., (1982). The Well and the Tree

Bellows, H. (Trans.) (1936). The Poetic Edda.

Berk, A., and Spytma, W., (2002) Penance, Power, and Pursuit, On the Trail of the Wild Hunt

Birley, Anthony R. (Trans.) (1999). Agricola and Germany

Blain, J., (2002). Nine Worlds of Seid-Magic

Bray, O., (1908) Poetic Edda

Byock, J., (1998) The Saga of King Hrolf Kraki

—(2005). The Prose Edda

Cameron, M., (1993). Anglo-Saxon Medicine.

Carmichael, A., (1900). Carmina Gadelica volume 2

Chisholm, J., (2002). Grove and Gallows

Crossley-Holland, K., (1981) The Norse Myths

Ellis, H., (1968) The Road to Hel

Ellis-Davidson, H., (1964). Gods and Myths of Northern Europe

—(1973). *"Hostile Magic in the Icelandic Sagas."* In: The Witch Figure: Folklore Essays by a Group of Scholars in England Honouring the 75th Birthday of Katharine M. Briggs

—(1988). Myths and Symbols in Pagan Europe

—(1993). The Lost Beliefs of Northern Europe

Ewing, T., (2008). Gods and Worshippers in the Viking and Germanic World

Ford, D., (2001). Royal Berkshire History: Beware the Ghostly Hunt

Fortson, B., (2004). Indo-European language and culture: an

introduction

Grimm, J., (1888). Teutonic Mythology, volume 1

—(1883) Teutonic Mythology volume 3

Grundy, S., (1995). The Cult of Odinn: God of Death?

—(1994). Miscellaneous Studies Towards the Cult of Odinn

Gundarsson, K., (2006). Our Troth, volume 1

—(2007) Our Troth vol 2

—(2007). Elves, Wights, and Trolls

Harper, D., (2016) Online Etymology Dictionary, 'Odin', retrieved
from http://www.etymonline.com/index.php?term=odin

Heinrichs, A., (nd). The Search for Identity: A Problem after the
conversion

Herbert, K., (1995). Looking for the Lost Gods of England

Hollander, L., (1936). Old Norse Poems: The Most Important
Nonskaldic Verse Not Included in the Poetic Edda

—(Trans.) (1964). Heimskringla

Hyllested, A., (2010) The Precursors of Celtic and Germanic

Jones, M (2003) The Wild Hunt. Retrieved from www.maryjones.
us/jce/wildhunt.html

Kershaw, K., (2000). The One-eyed God: Odin and the (Indo-)
Germanic Mannerbunde

Lafayllve, P., (2013). A Practical Heathen's Guide to Asatru

Larrington, C., (1996). The Poetic Edda

Lecouteux, C., (1999). Phantom Armies of the Night

O'Donoghue, H., (2008). From Asgard to Valhalla

Óðins nöfn (n.d.) Skaldic Poetry of the Scandinavian Middle
Ages http://skaldic.abdn.ac.uk/

Orchard, A., (1997) Dictionary of Norse Myth and Legend

Palson, H., (1972). Eyrbyggja Saga

Paxson, D., (2005) Taking Up the Runes

—(2006) Essential Asatru

—(2008) Trance-Portation

Pollington, S., (2003). The Mead-Hall: Feasting in Anglo-Saxon
England

Rowsell, T., (2012). Woden and His Roles in Anglo-Saxon Royal Genealogy

Scudder, B., (1997). Egil's Saga

Sigrdrifumal (n.d.) Retrieved from http://www.northvegr.org/the%20 eddas/the%20poetic%20edda%20%20-%20thorpe%20translation/ sigrdrifumal%20-%20the%20lay%20of%20sigrdrifa%20 page%201.html

Simek, R., (1993). Dictionary of Northern Mythology

Simpson, J., (1973). "Olaf Tryggvason versus the Powers of Darkness." In: The Witch Figure: Folklore Essays by a Group of Scholars in England Honouring the 75th Birthday of Katharine M. Briggs.

Tourville-Petre, E., (1964). Myth and Religion of the North

Towrie, S., (2013) The Wild Hunt.

Vafþrúðnismál (n. d.) Retrieved from http://www.northvegr.org/ the%20eddas/the%20poetic%20edda%20%20-%20thorpe%20 translation/vaf%C3%9Er%C3%BA%C3%B0nism%C3%A1l%20 -%20the%20lay%20of%20vafthrudnir.html

Young, J, (1964) Prose Edda

We think you will also enjoy…

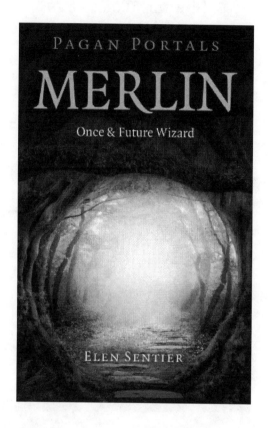

Merlin: Once and Future Wizard

Merlin in history, Merlin in mythology, Merlin through the ages
and his continuing relevance

*…a grand and imaginative work that introduces the reader to the many
faces of the mysterious Merlin.*
Morgan Daimler

978-1-78535-453-3 (paperback)
978-1-78535-454-0 (e-book)

Best Selling Pagan Portals
& Shaman Pathways

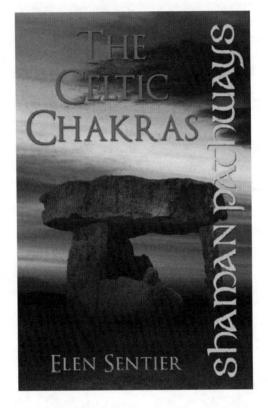

Celtic Chakras, Elen Sentier

Tread the British native shaman's path, explore the Goddess
hidden in the ancient stories; walk the Celtic chakra spiral
labyrinth.

Rich with personal vision, the book is an interesting exploration of
wholeness
Emma Restall Orr

978-1-78099-506-9 (paperback)
978-1-78099-507-6 (e-book)

Druid Shaman, Danu Forest

A practical guide to Celtic shamanism with exercises and
techniques as well as traditional lore for exploring the Celtic
Otherworld

*A sound, practical introduction to a complex and wide-ranging
subject*
Philip Shallcrass

978-1-78099-615-8 (paperback)
978-1-78099-616-5 (e-book)

Best Selling Pagan Portals
& Shaman Pathways

Kitchen Witchcraft, Rachel Patterson
Take a glimpse at the workings of a Kitchen Witch and
share in the crafts

*A wonderful little book which will get anyone started on Kitchen
Witchery. Informative, and easy to follow*
Janet Farrar & Gavin Bone

978-1-78099-843-5 (paperback)
978-1-78099-842-8 (e-book)

Moon Magic, Rachel Patterson

An introduction to working with the phases of the Moon

*...a delightful treasury of lore and spiritual musings that should be
essential to any planetary magic-worker's reading list.*
David Salisbury

978-1-78279-281-9 (paperback)
978-1-78279-282-6 (e-book)

Best Selling Pagan Portals & Shaman Pathways

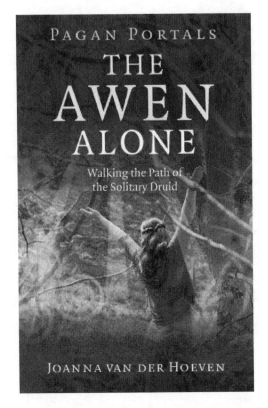

The Awen Alone, Joanna van der Hoeven
An introductory guide for the solitary Druid

Joanna's voice carries the impact and knowledge of the ancestors, combined with the wisdom of contemporary understanding.
Cat Treadwell

978-1-78279-547-6 (paperback)
978-1-78279-546-9 (e-book)

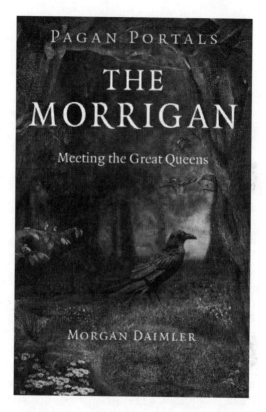

The Morrigan, Morgan Daimler

On shadowed wings and in raven's call, meet the ancient Irish
Goddess of war, battle, prophecy, death, sovereignty, and magic

*...a well-researched and heartfelt guide to the Morrigan from a fellow
devotee and priestess*
Stephanie Woodfield

978-1-78279-833-0 (paperback)
978-1-78279-834-7 (e-book)

MOON BOOKS

Moon Books

PAGANISM & SHAMANISM

What is Paganism? A religion, a spirituality, an alternative belief system, nature worship? You can find support for all these definitions (and many more) in dictionaries, encyclopaedias, and text books of religion, but subscribe to any one and the truth will evade you. Above all Paganism is a creative pursuit, an encounter with reality, an exploration of meaning and an expression of the soul. Druids, Heathens, Wiccans and others, all contribute their insights and literary riches to the Pagan tradition. Moon Books invites you to begin or to deepen your own encounter, right here, right now.

If you have enjoyed this book, why not tell other readers by posting a review on your preferred book site. Recent bestsellers from Moon Books are:

Journey to the Dark Goddess
How to Return to Your Soul
Jane Meredith
Discover the powerful secrets of the Dark Goddess and transform your depression, grief and pain into healing and integration.
Paperback: 978-1-84694-677-6 ebook: 978-1-78099-223-5

Shamanic Reiki
Expanded Ways of Working with Universal Life Force Energy
Llyn Roberts, Robert Levy
Shamanism and Reiki are each powerful ways of healing; together,
their power multiplies. Shamanic Reiki introduces techniques to
help healers and Reiki practitioners tap ancient healing wisdom.
Paperback: 978-1-84694-037-8 ebook: 978-1-84694-650-9

Pagan Portals – The Awen Alone
Walking the Path of the Solitary Druid
Joanna van der Hoeven
An introductory guide for the solitary Druid, The Awen Alone
will accompany you as you explore, and seek out your own place
within the natural world.
Paperback: 978-1-78279-547-6 ebook: 978-1-78279-546-9

A Kitchen Witch's World of Magical Herbs & Plants
Rachel Patterson
A journey into the magical world of herbs and plants, filled with
magical uses, folklore, history and practical magic. By popular
writer, blogger and kitchen witch, Tansy Firedragon.
Paperback: 978-1-78279-621-3 ebook: 978-1-78279-620-6

Medicine for the Soul
The Complete Book of Shamanic Healing
Ross Heaven
All you will ever need to know about shamanic healing and how to
become your own shaman...
Paperback: 978-1-78099-419-2 ebook: 978-1-78099-420-8

Shaman Pathways – The Druid Shaman
Exploring the Celtic Otherworld
Danu Forest
A practical guide to Celtic shamanism with exercises and
techniques as well as traditional lore for exploring the Celtic
Otherworld.
Paperback: 978-1-78099-615-8 ebook: 978-1-78099-616-5

Traditional Witchcraft for the Woods and Forests
A Witch's Guide to the Woodland with Guided Meditations and
Pathworking
Melusine Draco
A Witch's guide to walking alone in the woods, with guided
meditations and pathworking.
Paperback: 978-1-84694-803-9 ebook: 978-1-84694-804-6

Wild Earth, Wild Soul
A Manual for an Ecstatic Culture
Bill Pfeiffer
Imagine a nature-based culture so alive and so connected,
spreading like wildfire. This book is the first flame...
Paperback: 978-1-78099-187-0 ebook: 978-1-78099-188-7

Naming the Goddess
Trevor Greenfield
Naming the Goddess is written by over eighty adherents and
scholars of Goddess and Goddess Spirituality.
Paperback: 978-1-78279-476-9 ebook: 978-1-78279-475-2

Shapeshifting into Higher Consciousness
Heal and Transform Yourself and Our World with Ancient
Shamanic and Modern Methods
Llyn Roberts
Ancient and modern methods that you can use every day to
transform yourself and make a positive difference in the world.
Paperback: 978-1-84694-843-5 ebook: 978-1-84694-844-2

Readers of ebooks can buy or view any of these bestsellers by
clicking on the live link in the title. Most titles are published in
paperback and as an ebook. Paperbacks are available in traditional
bookshops. Both print and ebook formats are available online.

Find more titles and sign up to our readers' newsletter at http://
www.johnhuntpublishing.com/paganism
Follow us on Facebook at https://www.facebook.com/MoonBooks
and Twitter at https://twitter.com/MoonBooksJHP